# Great Chefs
# Great Chocolate

# Great Chefs
# Great Chocolate

## Spectacular Desserts from America's Great Chefs

From the television series GREAT CHEFS

*Edited by*

## Julia M. Pitkin

A Cumberland House *Hearthside* Book

### CUMBERLAND HOUSE

*Nashville, Tennessee*

Great Chefs® is a registered trademark of Great Chefs® Television/Publishing,
a division of GCI, Inc. Great Chefs® Trademark
Reg. U.S. Pat. Off. and in other countries.

A free catalog of other Great Chefs products is available.
Call 1-800-321-1499, or contact www.greatchefs.com.

Published by Cumberland House Publishing, Inc.,
431 Harding Industrial Drive
Nashville, Tennessee 37211

Design by Bruce Gore, Gore Studio, Inc., Nashville, Tennessee


**Library of Congress Cataloging-in-Publication Data**

Great chefs, great chocolate : spectacular desserts from Americas
    great chefs / edited by Julia M. Pitkin.
        p. cm.
    "Cumberland House hearthside book."
    Includes bibliographical references and index.
    ISBN 1–888952–83–0  (hardcover : alk. paper)
    1. Cookery (Chocolate)    2. Desserts.    3. Cooks—United States.
I. Pitkin, Julia M.
TX767.C5G743    1998
641.6'374—dc21                                98–28033
                                                CIP


Printed in the United States of America
1 2 3 4 5 6 7 — 01 00 99 98 97

# Contents

# Credits

Television Series

| | |
|---|---|
| Presenter | Mary Lou Conroy |
| Announcer | Andres Calandria |
| Editor/Animation | George Matulik |
| Assistant Editor | Maria D. Estevez |
| Post-Production Audio | Andres Calandria |
| | C. Caldwell Sainz |
| Original Music | The Charlie Byrd Quartet |
| Recording Studio | Ultrasonic Studios |
| Recording Engineer | Steve Reynolds |
| Additional Footage | Paul Cornbel |
| Transportation General | Bryan Dupepe |
| Assistant to the Executive Producer | |
| | Cybil W. Curtis |
| Producer/Director/Writer | |
| | John Beyer |
| Executive Producer | John Shoup |

Book

For Great Chefs

| | |
|---|---|
| Photography | Eric Futran |
| Project Coordinator | Linda Anne Nix |

# Acknowledgments

Many, many thanks to John Shoup for giving me this opportunity. My sincerest gratitude to Linda Nix, who helped with so many aspects of compiling this book, and is always gracious and accommodating of my every request.

This book would not be possible without the contributions of the many chefs who participated in the television series, and provided these wonderful recipes.

I would also like to thank the wonderful people at Cumberland House for their talents, support, and enthusiasm.

# Mail Order Sources

G. B. Ratto, International Grocers
821 Washington Street
Oakland, CA 94607
510-832-6503
Write for a catalog of their chocolate, nuts, flavor extracts, and spices.

Hawaiian Fruit Specialties, Ltd.
P.O. Box 637
Kahuku, HI 96731
808-332-9333
808-332-7650 fax
This retail supplier will mail island jams, jellies, mango chutney, and syrups.

Hawaiian Vintage Chocolate Company
4614 Kilauea Avenue, Suite 435
Honolulu, HI 96816
808-735-8494
High-quality white, semisweet, and dark chocolate produced on the Big Island of Hawaii. Available both wholesale and retail.

Kitchen Crafts, Inc.
2410 W. 79th Street
Merrillville, IN 46307
Confectionery and bakery supplies and tools.

Leonard Solomon's Wines and Spirits
L&L Distributing
1456 North Dayton
Chicago, IL 60622
312-915-5911
312-915-0466 fax
Many fine products, including crème fraîche, Amazon spices, frozen purées, and vanilla beans.

MacFarms of Hawaii
HC01, P.O. Box 3
Waialua, HI 96791
800-367-6010 or 808-637-5620
808-734-4675
Unsalted dry-roasted macadamia nuts and other macadamia products by mail.

Madame Chocolate
1940-C Lehigh Avenue
Glenview, IL 60025
The chocolate lady, Elaine Sherman, sells every brand of high-quality imported chocolates, including Mexican chocolate.

Sweet Celebrations
P.O. Box 39426
Edina, MN 55439
1-800-328-6722
612-943-1688
A complete catalog of confectioners' supplies, including chocolate and other ingredients, and equipment.

Take Home Maui
121 Dickenson Street
Lahaina, HI 96761
808-661-8067
A mail order source for fresh pineapple, papaya, and macadamia products.

Albert Uster Imports, Inc.
9211 Gaither Road
Gaithersburg, MD 20877
1-800-231-8154
A professional source for confectionery and bakery supplies and tools, including edible gold dust.

White Lily Flour Company
P.O. Box 871
Knoxville, TN 37901
Soft-wheat flour to use for southern biscuits or in place of cake flour for cakes.

Wilton Enterprises, Inc.
2240 West 75th Street
Woodridge, IL 60515
708-963-7100, ext. 320
Pastry and cake decorating supples, paste food colors, and icing ingredients.

# Introduction

## The Temptation of Chocolate

For years I have enjoyed watching the Great Chefs® television series, so when we first began discussing the possibility of publishing a collection of chocolate recipes from the series, I enthusiastically offered to create and edit the book myself. Not only am I among the millions of people who sit up and take notice at the mention of chocolate, as editor in chief of Cumberland House Hearthside Books I have long looked forward to publishing a chocolate book. Where would I ever find a better selection of chocolate recipes than at Great Chefs®? Equally tempting was the bounty of wonderful photographs of chocolate masterpieces available from the producer of the series.

I was hooked on the project from the beginning. What you now hold in your hands is the result of a long process of reviewing the recipes as they were prepared on television, testing them for taste and accuracy, making sure they were written clearly, and being sure that the methods produce food as delicious as it looks on television.

The recipes in this book come from restaurants from every region of the United States as well as the Caribbean. There are wonderful recipes for milk chocolate masterpieces, white chocolate delicacies, and—now we're arriving at my favorites—heavenly dark or bittersweet chocolate treasures. Included are recipes for every level of culinary ability, from cookies and brownies to gravity-defying tortes and soufflés, and from cakes and pies to molded and sculpted desserts requiring a trip to the hardware store—that's right, the hardware store! For the health-conscious cook, Chef Kathleen Daelemans has even provided a couple of fabulous low-fat recipes.

As a practical matter, anyone planning to enjoy the culinary skills of any of the chefs represented in this book should call before making a special trip to enjoy their food. Some of the chefs are no longer at the restaurants where they were working when their segments were filmed. Some have moved on to new venues, and a quick call might just save you some disappointment. Addresses and telephone numbers of all the restaurants in the book are listed on pages 203-205.

It is often said that we Southerners have a sweet tooth. Without question, dessert is my favorite course and baking my favorite reason to be in the kitchen. Chocolate, however, lifts my love of wonderful desserts to a new level. For me, it can't be too dark or too rich. Since you are holding this cookbook, you probably take chocolate seriously too. Do you keep the phone numbers for chocolate shops across the nation in your Rolodex? Do you ever make a New Year's resolution to eat chocolate every day of the year? (Like it wouldn't happen anyway!)

If so, this is the book for you. Assuming you can restrain yourself from snacking on the chocolate before you start cooking with it, you will be satisfied with the results you get with these recipes. The tastes, the textures—Mmmm!

Don't just take my word for it.

—Julia M. Pitkin
Editor in Chief
Cumberland House Hearthside Books

# Great Chefs®
# Great Chocolate

# Cakes

## Chocolate Banana Foster Cake with Orange Foster Caramel Sauce

*Will Greenwood*
SUNSET GRILL
NASHVILLE, TENNESSEE

**SERVES 8**

### CHOCOLATE BANANA CAKE:

| | |
|---|---|
| 2 | cups all-purpose flour |
| 1 | tablespoon baking powder |
| ⅓ | cup cocoa |
| ⅓ | cup (5 tablespoons) unsalted butter, at room temperature |
| 2 | cups sugar |
| 3 | large eggs |

### MOUSSE:

| | |
|---|---|
| 1 | teaspoon gelatin |
| ⅓ | cup banana rum |
| 1 | cup mashed bananas |
| ½ | cup heavy (whipping) cream |
| ⅓ | cup sugar |

### CHOCOLATE GANACHE:

| | |
|---|---|
| ⅓ | cup heavy (whipping) cream |
| 2 | tablespoons corn syrup |
| ½ | pound semisweet chocolate pieces |

### ORANGE FOSTER CARAMEL SAUCE:

| | |
|---|---|
| ½ | cup sugar |
| ¼ | cup water |
| ¼ | cup Grand Marnier |
| ½ | cup orange juice |
| 2 | teaspoons lemon juice |
| 3 | tablespoons butter |
| | Puff pastry rounds |
| 2 | whole bananas, sliced |
| ¼ | cup sugar |
| | Grand Marnier |
| 3 | cups vanilla ice cream |
| | Orange zest |
| | Fresh mint |

*To make the chocolate banana foster cake:* Preheat the oven to 350F°. Butter a cookie sheet and dust lightly with flour, tapping out the excess. Sift together the flour, baking powder, and cocoa. In the bowl of an electric mixer combine the butter and sugar and mix on medium-high speed until creamy. Add the eggs one at a time, beating well after each addition. Add the dry ingredients and blend well. Spoon the batter onto the prepared pan, smooth the top with a rubber spatula, and bake in the preheated oven about 20 minutes until a toothpick inserted in the center is clean when removed. Let the cake cool in the pan, set on a wire rack, for 10 minutes. (The cake can be made up to 3 days ahead.) When the cake is cooled, cut enough rounds to cover the bottom, sides, and top of individual 6-inch round molds.

*To make the banana mousse:* In a small bowl sprinkle the gelatin over the banana rum, and let rest for 5 minutes. Place this mixture over hot water in the top of a double boiler, and heat until it melts. In the bowl of a food processor purée the bananas. Gradually add the puréed bananas to the gelatin. In the well-chilled bowl of an electric mixer fitted with a chilled balloon whip, beat the heavy cream on high speed about 1 minute until peaks just begin to form. With the mixer on low speed, add the sugar and whip about 2 minutes until soft peaks form. Be careful not to overwhip or the mousse will be grainy. Add the whipped cream to the bananas by gently folding in the cream ½ cup at a time.

*To make the chocolate ganache:* In a medium saucepan combine the cream and corn syrup and bring to a boil over medium heat. Remove the pan from the heat and add the chocolate pieces, stirring until the chocolate is melted and the mixture is smooth and shiny.

*To make the orange foster caramel sauce:* In a medium saucepan bring the sugar and water to a boil over medium heat, and cook about 8 minutes or until the mixture reaches a light brown color and a caramel is formed. Remove the pan from the heat, add the Grand Marnier, orange juice, lemon juice, and the butter, and return the mixture to the stove. Bring to a slow boil over low heat, and cook about 1 minute until the mixture becomes liquid again.

*To make the puff pastry:* Preheat the oven to 350F°. Grease a large sheet with softened butter. With a rolling pin, roll the puff pastry until thin and place on the prepared pan. Cover the pastry with a second clean cookie sheet in order to prevent the pastry from rising. Cook in the preheated oven for 5 minutes or until golden. Remove the pastry from the oven and allow to cool. Top each round with 5 banana slices, and sprinkle with 1 tablespoon of sugar. Place the pastry under the broiler for about 4 minutes or until the sugar just begins to caramelize.

*To assemble:* Line the bottom and sides of the molds with cake rounds. Sprinkle the cake with 1 tablespoon of Grand Marnier. Fill the molds with the banana mousse, placing it inside the cake. Place a final piece of cake on top of the mousse, sprinkling again with Grand Marnier, and refrigerate the molds about 30 minutes or until set. Unmold the individual molds by turning upside down onto a rack set over waxed paper. Pour the chocolate ganache over the "bombes" until completely covered. Refrigerate about 45 minutes to 1 hour or until set.

Cut the bombes in half, place one half on each individual dessert plate. Place a banana-topped puff pastry round on top of each serving. Pour ¼ cup of the orange foster sauce around the bombe, and finish with a 4-ounce scoop of ice cream on top. Garnish with 2 strips of orange zest and a sprig of fresh mint.

# Chocolate Cake

*Kathleen Daelemans*
CAFE KULA
GRAND WAILEA RESORT, WAILEA, MAUI

**SERVES 12**

A rich prune flavor comes through in this dense chocolate cake made with only 1 tablespoon of oil. The bright drizzles of fruit purée add eye appeal and an intense flavor boost.

CAKE:

| | |
|---|---|
| 1 | cup chocolate liqueur |
| 1 | cup pitted prunes |
| 1 | cup sugar |
| 1 | cup nonfat milk |
| 1 | tablespoon canola oil |
| 1 | tablespoon white wine vinegar |
| 1 | teaspoon vanilla extract |
| 1¼ | cups unbleached all-purpose flour |
| ⅓ | cup unsweetened cocoa |

| | |
|---|---|
| 1 | tablespoon ground espresso or instant espresso powder |
| 1 | teaspoon baking soda |

GARNISH:

| | |
|---|---|
| 1 | cup Raspberry Purée (page 187) |
| 1 | cup Passion Fruit Purée (page 187) |
| 4 | ounces white chocolate, melted |
| 4 | ounces bittersweet chocolate, melted |

*To make the cake:* Line the bottom of a 9-inch springform pan with parchment or waxed paper and coat with vegetable oil cooking spray. In a small saucepan, combine the liqueur and prunes and simmer over low heat for 20 minutes. Set aside and let cool to room temperature. Transfer to a blender or food processor and blend until smooth.

Preheat the oven to 350°F. In a large bowl combine the prune purée, sugar, milk, oil, vinegar, and vanilla. In a medium bowl combine the flour, cocoa, espresso, and baking soda. Add the dry ingredients to the prune mixture in fourths, stirring until completely blended. The batter will be thick.

Pour the batter into the prepared pan and bake for 30 to 40 minutes or until a toothpick inserted in the center comes out clean. Remove the cake from the oven and let cool for 10 minutes. Remove the sides from the pan, set the pan on a wire rack, and let cool completely.

*To serve:* Place the sauces and melted chocolates in squeeze bottles. Drizzle each dessert plate with the purées and the bittersweet chocolate. Place a slice of cake on each plate. Drizzle the melted white chocolate over each slice.

# Chocolate Cake with Roasted-Banana Sauce

*Robert Del Grande*

CAFE ANNIE
HOUSTON, TEXAS

**SERVES 8**

CAKE:

¾   cup (1½ sticks) unsalted butter, at room temperature
1⅓  cups sugar
3   egg yolks
1⅓  cups milk
⅓   cup heavy (whipping) cream
1   teaspoon vanilla extract
6   ounces semisweet chocolate, chopped
2   eggs
1½  cups cake flour
1   teaspoon baking powder
½   teaspoon salt

BANANA SAUCE:

4   ripe bananas
2   tablespoons dark rum
¼   to ½ cup sugar
1   cup heavy (whipping) cream
1   teaspoon vanilla extract

GARNISH:

Banana slices
Mint sprigs
Pecan halves

❧ *To make the cake:* Preheat the oven to 350°F. Butter the sides and bottom of a deep-sided 10-inch round cake pan or springform pan. Line the bottom with parchment paper, butter the parchment paper, and lightly dust with flour. In the bowl of an electric mixer combine the butter and 1 cup of the sugar and beat about 15 minutes at low speed until the butter loses its yellow color.

In the top of a double boiler combine the egg yolks, ⅓ cup of the milk, the cream, and vanilla. Whisk together and then stir with a wooden spoon over simmering water until the custard thickens and coats the back of a spoon; do not allow it to boil or the egg yolks will curdle. Remove from the heat and stir in the chocolate. Allow to cool.

Add the whole eggs one at a time to the butter mixture. Then add the chocolate custard. Sift the dry ingredients together and add to the mixture alternately with the remaining 1 cup of milk. When the batter is smooth, pour into the prepared pan. Place the pan in a larger baking pan, add hot water to halfway up the sides of the cake pan, and bake in the center of the preheated oven for 60 to 70 minutes.

Cool on a rack for 10 minutes. Remove the cake from the pan and place on a wire rack.

❧ *To make the banana sauce:* Place the bananas in a 350°F oven for 20 minutes. Peel the bananas and place the pulp in a mixing bowl. Mash with a spoon, then add rum, sugar, cream, and vanilla.

✍ *To serve:* Spoon the sauce over the warm cake and garnish with slices of fresh banana, a sprig of mint, and a pecan half if desired.

✍ *Note:* The cake is best if baked just prior to serving; however, a cooled cake can be heated slightly in a 100F° oven before serving.

# Triple Chocolate Cake

*Curtis Young*
DALLAS, TEXAS

**SERVES 10 TO 12**

## CAKE:

| | |
|---|---|
| 2 | cups all-purpose flour |
| 2 | cups sugar |
| 3/4 | cup cocoa, plus extra to dust cake pans |
| 1½ | teaspoons baking soda |
| 1½ | teaspoons baking powder |
| 1 | teaspoon salt |
| 1 | cup milk |
| ½ | cup vegetable oil |
| 2 | eggs |
| 2 | teaspoons vanilla extract |
| 1 | ripe banana, mashed |
| ½ | cup sugar-coated chopped dates |
| ½ | cup boiling water |

## TOPPING:

| | |
|---|---|
| ¼ | cup sugar |
| ½ | cup semisweet chocolate chips |
| ½ | cup chopped nuts |

## FROSTING:

| | |
|---|---|
| ¾ | cup butter, softened |
| 3 | cups confectioners' sugar |
| ½ | cup cocoa |
| ¼ | cup milk |
| ½ | teaspoon vanilla extract |

## FILLING:

| | |
|---|---|
| 1 | 3-ounce package cream cheese, softened |
| ¼ | to ½ cup confectioners' sugar |
| 2 | tablespoons butter, softened |
| 1 | tablespoon vanilla extract |
| 2 | tablespoons cocoa |

## GARNISH:

Nut halves

*To make the cake:* Preheat the oven to 350°F. Grease two 9-inch round cake pans and dust with cocoa. In a mixing bowl sift the dry ingredients together. In a separate bowl mix the milk, oil, and eggs. Beat the liquid mixture into the dry ingredients. Add the vanilla, then stir in the mashed banana and chopped dates. Pour the boiling water into the batter and mix well. Divide the batter among the prepared pans.

*To make the topping:* In a small bowl combine the sugar, chocolate chips, and chopped nuts. Sprinkle the mixture over the top of the batter, pressing it in lightly.

Bake the cakes for 35 minutes or until a toothpick inserted in the center comes out clean. Cool for 10 minutes. Remove the cakes from the pans, and cool completely on wire racks.

*To make the frosting:* In a large bowl cream the butter with 1 cup of the sugar. Add the remaining sugar, cocoa, milk, and vanilla, and beat until smooth.

🍞 *To make the filling:* In a medium bowl beat the cream cheese with the sugar, butter, vanilla, and cocoa.

🍞 *To assemble the cake:* Place 1 cake layer on a large plate and spread with the filling. Place the second layer on top, then frost the sides and top with the frosting. Garnish with the nut halves.

# Fearrington House Chocolate Refresh-Mint

### Heather Mendenhall

FEARRINGTON HOUSE
PITTSBORO, NORTH CAROLINA

**SERVES 8**

CHOCOLATE CAKE:

| | |
|---|---|
| 2 | whole eggs |
| 2 | egg yolks |
| 1/2 | cup sugar |
| 1/3 | cup cake flour |
| 1/4 | teaspoon baking powder |
| | Pinch salt |
| 1/4 | cup melted butter |
| 1/4 | cup cocoa |

MINT JULEP SIMPLE SYRUP:

| | |
|---|---|
| 1/2 | cup sugar |
| 1 | cup water |
| 1/2 | cup fresh mint, chopped |
| 1/4 | cup bourbon |

MINTED CHOCOLATE MOUSSE:

| | |
|---|---|
| 1/4 | cup water |
| 1/2 | cup sugar |

| | |
|---|---|
| 2 | egg whites |
| 1 1/2 | cups sour cream |
| 1 | cup heavy (whipping) cream |
| 6 | ounces bittersweet chocolate |
| 1/4 | cup bourbon |
| 2 | tablespoons mint extract |

CHOCOLATE GANACHE GLAZE:

| | |
|---|---|
| 4 | ounces bittersweet chocolate |
| 1 | cup sour cream |
| 2 | tablespoons light corn syrup |
| 1/4 | cup bourbon |

GARNISH:

| | |
|---|---|
| 10 | sprigs fresh mint, finely chopped |

❧ *To make the chocolate cake:* Preheat the oven to 350°F. Line the bottom of a greased 10½-inch springform pan with waxed paper, grease the paper, and dust the pan with flour, knocking out the excess. In the large bowl of an electric mixer beat the eggs and yolks with the sugar on high speed for 5 minutes or until the mixture is pale yellow and forms a ribbon when the beaters are lifted. In a separate bowl sift the flour, baking powder, and salt together. Fold the dry ingredients into the egg mixture until the batter is just combined. In a small saucepan set over low heat melt the butter and cocoa together. Fold the chocolate-butter mixture gently but thoroughly into the flour mixture. Pour the batter into the pan, smoothing the top. Bake the cake in the middle of the oven for 20 minutes or until a tester comes out clean.

Transfer the cake to a rack, run a sharp knife around the edge, and remove the side of the pan. Invert the cake onto another rack and remove the waxed paper. Reinvert the cake onto the rack and let it cool completely. Clean the springform pan; it will be needed later to assemble the Refresh-Mint.

᪥ *To make the mint julep simple syrup:* In a medium, heavy-bottomed saucepan bring the sugar, water, chopped mint, and bourbon to a boil over medium-high heat. As soon as the mixture has come to a boil, remove the pan from the heat. Strain through a fine-mesh strainer and reserve.

᪥ *To make the minted chocolate mousse:* In a small saucepan combine the water and sugar and bring to a boil over medium heat. Continue cooking until the syrup has thickened and has large bubbles. In the well-chilled bowl of an electric mixer fitted with a balloon whisk, beat the egg whites at medium speed until soft peaks begin to form. Switch the speed to high and add the simple syrup. Whip until cool and stiff peaks have formed, about 5 minutes. Remove the meringue to a clean mixing bowl.

In a separate bowl combine the sour cream with the heavy cream and beat until soft peaks form. Place the chocolate in the top of a double boiler over hot water. Stir the chocolate until melted. Add the bourbon and mint extract to the chocolate, and let cool slightly. Fold into the cream mixture. Gently but thoroughly fold the chocolate mixture into the meringue.

᪥ *To make the chocolate ganache glaze:* Finely chop the chocolate and place in a clean mixing bowl. In a heavy-bottomed saucepan bring the sour cream, corn syrup, and bourbon to a boil over medium heat. Stir to combine. Pour this mixture over the chocolate and allow to rest 2 to 3 minutes before stirring. This will allow the chocolate to melt. With a rubber spatula, stir gently to combine.

᪥ *To assemble:* Cut the top of the cake to level it, and cut horizontally into 2 even layers. Place one layer of the cake into the cleaned springform pan and sprinkle with ½ cup of mint julep simple syrup. Once the syrup is absorbed, spread the cake layer with chocolate mousse until it reaches halfway up the pan. Top with second layer and sprinkle with syrup as before. Top with the remaining chocolate mousse, smoothing with a rubber spatula. Freeze the mousse cake for 1 hour. Remove from the freezer and spread chocolate ganache on top. Garnish with finely chopped fresh mint leaves. To remove from the pan, wrap a damp, hot towel around the pan for 1 minute, and release the sides. Smooth the sides of the cake with a rubber spatula.

# Warm Center Chocolate Pyramid Cake

Gene Bjorkand
AUBERGINE
MEMPHIS, TENNESSEE

**SERVES 6**

Because the chocolate cakes need to freeze 24 hours before they can be baked, this dessert takes some advance planning.

NUGGETS:

| | |
|---|---|
| 5 | ounces semisweet chocolate |
| ¼ | cup (½ stick) butter |
| 1 | cup heavy (whipping) cream |
| ½ | cup plus 2 tablespoons water |

CHOCOLATE CAKE:

| | |
|---|---|
| 2 | eggs, separated |
| ¼ | teaspoon cream of tartar |
| ¼ | teaspoon salt |
| ½ | cup sugar |
| 4 | ounces semisweet chocolate |

| | |
|---|---|
| 3 | tablespoons cake flour, sifted |
| 3 | tablespoons butter, at room temperature |
| 3 | tablespoons almond powder |
| 6 | tablespoons sugar |

CHOCOLATE SAUCE:

| | |
|---|---|
| 5 | tablespoons sugar |
| 7 | tablespoons water |
| 2 | tablespoons cocoa |
| ¼ | cup heavy (whipping) cream |

*Confectioners' sugar for dusting cakes*

*To make the nuggets:* In a heavy-bottomed saucepan melt the chocolate and butter with the cream and water over low heat. Mix gently until well combined and pour into a small ice cube tray. Freeze for 24 hours. While the nuggets are freezing, proceed with the cake recipe and let the cake remain in the refrigerator until you are ready to complete the dessert.

*To make the chocolate cake:* Lightly butter and dust with flour six 4-ounce cupcake molds or cups in a muffin tin. Separate the eggs. Place the egg whites, cream of tartar, and salt in the bowl of an electric mixer fitted with a balloon whip. On high speed whisk until soft peaks form. In a steady stream add the sugar and continue beating on high speed until stiff. Melt the chocolate in the top of a double boiler over simmering water. While maintaining a very low heat, gradually add the cake flour, mixing until a paste is formed. Add the softened butter, mixing until it is well incorporated. Mix in the almond powder and sugar. Remove the pan from the heat and add the egg yolks. Gently fold in the egg whites, and set aside. The cake batter will be somewhat grainy. Fill the prepared molds with the cake batter. Place the frozen nuggets in the center of each mold (not the bottom) and let the molds rest in the freezer 24 hours before baking.

*To make the chocolate sauce:* In a medium saucepan combine the sugar, water, cocoa, and cream, and simmer over low heat for 30 minutes. Remove the pan from the heat and transfer to a clean container. Cover and chill for 24 hours.

❧ *To assemble:* Preheat the oven to 350°F. Place the cake molds in the upper third of the oven and bake for 15 minutes or until firm. While the molds are baking, decorate individual dessert plates with the chocolate sauce. The chef likes to serve the sauce cold to contrast with the warm cakes but, if you prefer, the sauce may be warmed slowly over a low heat. Remove the cakes from the oven and let cool on a rack. To remove the cakes from the molds, carefully run a sharp knife around the inner edge of the mold and invert onto dessert plates. Sprinkle with confectioners' sugar.

# Kona Coffee and Hawaiian Vintage Chocolate Mousse Torte

### Gale E. O'Malley

HILTON HAWAIIAN VILLAGE
HONOLULU, OAHU

**SERVES 8**

This masterpiece is an exotic version of a layer cake: chocolate layers, a meringue layer, two flavors of mousse, and marzipan, garnished with Hawaiian poho berries. Standing the cake wedges up vertically makes a dramatic presentation. The meringue mushrooms could garnish almost any dessert.

### MARZIPAN DISK:

| | |
|---|---|
| ½ | pound marzipan |
| 3 | drops green food coloring |

### MERINGUE DISK AND MUSHROOMS:

| | |
|---|---|
| 6 | egg whites |
| ½ | teaspoon cream of tartar |
| 1½ | cups confectioners' sugar, sifted |
| ¾ | cup macadamia nuts, finely ground |
| | Unsweetened cocoa for dusting |

### CHOCOLATE CAKE:

| | |
|---|---|
| 4 | eggs |
| ⅔ | cup sugar |
| ¼ | cup cocoa |
| | Pinch salt |
| ¾ | cup cake flour, sifted |
| 3 | tablespoons unsalted butter, melted |
| ¼ | cup apricot jam |
| 1 | cup Ganache (page 185) |

### KONA COFFEE MOUSSE:

| | |
|---|---|
| 3 | envelopes plain gelatin |
| 4 | tablespoons instant coffee powder |
| ½ | cup water |
| 2 | cups heavy (whipping) cream |
| 5 | egg yolks |
| ¾ | cup confectioners' sugar, sifted |
| ¼ | cup Kahlua |

### HAWAIIAN VINTAGE CHOCOLATE MOUSSE:

| | |
|---|---|
| 6 | ounces Hawaiian Vintage Chocolate or other fine-quality bittersweet chocolate |
| 3 | envelopes plain gelatin |
| ½ | cup water |
| 2 | cups heavy (whipping) cream |
| 5 | egg yolks |
| ¾ | cup confectioners' sugar, sifted |
| 4 | ounces bittersweet chocolate, melted |
| ½ | cup Raspberry Purée (page 187) |
| 24 | fresh poho berries or raspberries |
| 8 | fresh mint sprigs |

   *To make the marzipan disk:* Knead the marzipan until pliable. Dot with 3 drops of green food coloring, fold the marzipan over the coloring, and knead until the color has spread evenly throughout the marzipan. On a piece of parchment paper or aluminum foil, roll the marzipan into a 9-inch round disk that is ⅛ inch thick. Press with the back of a large knife to score the disk with parallel lines ¼ inch apart. Refrigerate.

❧ *To make the meringue disk and mushrooms:* Preheat the oven to 200°F. Line a baking sheet with parchment or buttered heavy brown paper. Trace around a 9-inch round cake pan to draw a circle on the paper. In a large bowl beat the egg whites and cream of tartar together until stiff peaks form. Gradually add the confectioners' sugar, beating until stiff peaks form. Place one-fourth of the meringue in a pastry bag fitted with a medium plain tip. On the edges of the prepared baking sheets, outside the traced circle, pipe sixteen ¾-inch puffs (for the mushroom caps) and 16 thin 1½-inch lines (for mushroom stems) on the prepared baking sheet. Put any leftover meringue back into the bowl with the reserved meringue anf fold in the macadamia nut flour. Place the nut meringue in a large pastry bag fitted with a large plain tip and pipe in a tight spiral on the circle drawn on the prepared baking sheet. Fill in the circle with meringue and smooth the top slightly with a spatula or table knife. Bake for 1 hour to 1 hour and 30 minutes until crisp but not browned. Remove from the oven, lift the paper with the meringues, and place on a wire rack to cool right on the paper.

When cool, lift from the paper. With a sharp knife, trim the meringue circle to fit inside the cake pan. Set aside. With the tip of a sharp knife, scrape a small hole in the bottom of each mushroom cap. Use the same knife to shave one end of each stem into a small point. Press a stem point into each cap. Dust the caps with a little cocoa powder and set aside.

❧ *To make the cake:* Preheat the oven to 350°F. Line the bottoms of two 9-inch round cake pans with parchment paper. Warm a deep bowl by filling the bowl with warm water, emptying it, and drying it thoroughly. In the warmed bowl, beat the eggs and sugar together until the mixture thickens and a ribbon forms when a spoonful is drizzled on the surface. Fold the cocoa into the egg mixture. Gradually fold the salt and two-thirds of the flour into the egg mixture. Blend a large spoonful of the mixture into the butter, then gently fold the butter and remaining one-third of the flour into the mixture. Pour into the prepared pans and bake for 10 minutes or until a toothpick inserted in the center comes out clean. Let the cakes cool in the pan for 10 minutes, then remove the cakes to a wire rack to cool completely. You will have two ½-inch thick cakes.

Line a 9x2-inch round cake pan with a circle of parchment paper or greased waxed paper. Cut a strip of heavy flexible plastic 4 inches wide and 30 inches long. Place the plastic strip around the inside of the cake pan, letting it extend above the top.

In a small pan melt the jam over medium heat. Strain the jam through a fine-mesh sieve. Spread a thin layer of about one-third of the apricot jam on one cake circle and place in the prepared pan jam side up. Place the ganache in a pastry bag fitted with a large plain tip and pipe a spiral of ganache over the jam.

❧ *To make the coffee mousse:* In a small bowl sprinkle the gelatin and instant coffee over the water and set aside. In a deep bowl beat the cream until soft peaks form and set aside. In a large bowl whip the egg yolks and sugar until the mixture thickens and a slowly dissolving ribbon forms when a spoonful is drizzled on the surface. Stir in the gelatin mixture and blend until completely dissolved. Stir one-fourth of the whipped cream into the egg mixture to lighten it, then fold in the remaining cream. Pour over the ganache in the cake pan, and smooth the top.

Place the meringue disk over the coffee mousse, pressing it slightly into the mousse to bond. Sprinkle the Kahlua over the meringue disk.

*To make the chocolate mousse:* In a double boiler over simmering water melt the chocolate. Set aside in the pan. In a small bowl sprinkle the gelatin over the water and set aside. In a deep bowl whip the cream until it forms soft peaks and set aside. In a large bowl whip the egg yolks and sugar until the mixture thickens and a slowly dissolving ribbon forms when a spoonful is drizzled on the surface. Stir in the gelatin mixture and blend until completely dissolved. With a rubber spatula, gently stir in the warm chocolate. Stir one-fourth of the whipped cream into the egg mixture to lighten the mixture, then fold in the remaining cream. Pour over the meringue disk in the cake pan and smooth the top.

Spread the second cake circle with one-third of the apricot jam and place jam side down over the mousse, pressing it slightly into the mousse to bond. Spread the remaining apricot jam over the top of the cake. Press the marzipan disk into the jam scored side up. Place the cake in the freezer for 1 to 2 hours or until frozen.

*To serve:* Remove the cake from the freezer. Turn the cake out of the pan and remove the paper from the bottom. Place the cake on a serving plate. Gently pull the plastic strip off the side. With a heavy sharp knife cut the cake into wedges, dipping the knife in hot water and wiping the blade between cuts. With a pastry brush or smaller spoon, cover one-half of the top of each wedge with melted chocolate. Place 2 dots of melted chocolate off center on each plate and stand a meringue mushroom on each dot, holding the mushrooms until the chocolate cools and they stand upright on their own. With a spatula and your hand, lift each cake wedge and place it upright on its spine on each serving plate next to the mushrooms. Spoon a little raspberry purée on each plate. Remove the husks from 16 poho berries and spread open the husks on the remaining 8 poho berries. Garnish each plate with 2 husked berries, 1 berry with the husk still attached, and 1 mint sprig.

# A Riot in Chocolate

*Richard Leach*

GOTHAM BAR AND GRILL
NEW YORK, NEW YORK

**MAKES 6 INDIVIDUAL CAKES**

This dessert combines chocolate in all its most luscious forms: creamy mousse, tender cake, ice cream, and crisp cookies. The tea flavoring in the ice cream adds an unusual and delicious note to the dramatic dessert. The chef uses Valrhona chocolate, but any high-quality imported chocolate may be used.

CHOCOLATE MOUSSE:

| | |
|---|---|
| 8 | ounces Valrhona extra-bitter chocolate, chopped |
| ½ | cup milk |
| 2 | egg yolks |
| 1½ | tablespoons sugar |
| ½ | cup (1 stick) unsalted butter, melted |
| 2 | cups heavy (whipping) cream |

CHOCOLATE CAKE:

| | |
|---|---|
| 1 | cup (2 sticks) unsalted butter, at room temperature |
| 2¾ | cups sugar |
| 1 | cup unsweetened cocoa |
| 3 | eggs |
| 3½ | cups cake flour |

| | |
|---|---|
| 1½ | teaspoons baking powder |
| 1½ | teaspoons baking soda |
| 1 | teaspoon salt |
| 2 | cups warm water |

CHOCOLATE-TEA ICE CREAM:

| | |
|---|---|
| 4 | cups heavy (whipping) cream |
| 2 | cups milk |
| 8 | Earl Grey tea bags |
| 1½ | cups sugar |
| 12 | egg yolks |
| 8 | ounces Valrhona extra-bitter chocolate |

*Fresh mint sprigs*
*Chocolate Tuile Cookies (page 19)*

*To make the chocolate mousse:* In a large bowl combine the chocolate and milk. In a large saucepan bring 1 inch of water to a simmer and place the bowl on top. Stir until the chocolate is melted, then remove the bowl and keep the chocolate mixture warm.

In another large bowl combine the egg yolks and sugar. Place the bowl over the pan of simmering water and beat until the eggs are warmed. Remove from the heat and beat until the egg mixture is pale and thick. Gradually add the melted chocolate and melted butter to the eggs, mixing just until incorporated. Remove from the heat and keep warm.

In a deep bowl whip the cream until it forms soft peaks. Fold the whipped cream gently into the chocolate mixture until fully incorporated. Place the mousse in a clean bowl, cover, and refrigerate until needed.

*To make the chocolate cake:* Butter an 8-inch round cake pan and set aside. Preheat the oven to 300°F. In the bowl of an electric mixer combine the butter and sugar and beat with the paddle attachment for about 5 minutes or until the mixture is light and fluffy. Stop the machine and add the cocoa. Mix at low speed and slowly add the eggs, one at a time. Mix until smooth. Sift the flour, baking powder, baking soda, and salt together. Add all at once to the cocoa mixture and mix until smooth at low speed, scraping the sides of the bowl as necessary. Slowly add the warm water. Scrape the batter into the prepared cake pan and bake for 20 to 25 minutes or until the cake is firm and springy to the touch. Cool the cake in the pan on a wire rack for 10 minutes, then remove the cake from the pan and let cool completely. Cover and refrigerate.

    *To make the chocolate-tea ice cream:* In a large, heavy saucepan combine the heavy cream, milk, tea bags, and 1 cup of sugar. Bring the mixture to a boil over medium heat. Remove the pan from heat and let the tea steep for 20 minutes. Place the egg yolks and the remaining ½ cup of sugar in a medium bowl and stir to combine. Strain the tea-infused cream into a clean pot and bring to a full boil over medium heat. Quickly whisk the boiling liquid into the yolks and sugar. Immediately add the chopped chocolate, stirring the mixture until smooth. Strain through a fine-mesh sieve into a clean mixing bowl. Place the bowl of chocolate mixture inside another bowl filled with ice. Once the custard is cold, transfer the mixture to an ice cream maker and freeze according to the manufacturer's instructions.

    *To assemble the mousse cakes:* You will need six 3x1½ inch ring molds, a pastry bag with a No. 8 tip, and a 1- inch diameter round cutter. Cut the cake into very thin (about ¼ inch) crosswise slices. Using the metal rings, cut out 12 disks of cake. Place a cake disk at the bottom of each ring mold. Fill the pastry bag with the chocolate mousse. Pipe chocolate mousse into the rings until it reaches ½ inch up the side of each mold. Smooth the mousse flat with a tablespoon dipped in hot water. Place a second disk of chocolate cake on top of the chocolate mousse, creating a sandwich. Press down until level and flat. Refrigerate for about 1 hour until firm.
    When each mousse cake is firm, remove it from the refrigerator. Dip the smaller 1-inch round cutter in hot water and cut a hole slightly off center in the chocolate sandwich. Remove the mousse cakes from the ring molds by rubbing each ring with your hands until the cake is released. Carefully push it out of the ring mold and refrigerate.

    *To make the chocolate wrapping:* Preheat the oven to 300°F. In a double boiler over barely simmering water melt the chocolate, stirring until smooth. Set aside. Place a baking sheet in the preheated oven until it is very warm, about 30 to 45 seconds. Remove the pan from the oven and spread the melted chocolate onto the back of the sheet pan in a very thin, even layer. Place the pan in the freezer or refrigerator for 1 hour. Remove the pan and let sit at room temperature until the chocolate is warm enough to peel off the sheet pan using a paring knife, about 5 minutes. Cut 9-inch long by 1-inch wide strips of chocolate and peel off the pan. Carefully wrap a strip of chocolate around the sides of each disk of mousse cake (so that it looks like a smooth frosting). Wrap all 6 mousse cakes and refrigerate.

    *To serve:* Place one of the chocolate mousse cakes on each plate, add a scoop of the chocolate-tea ice cream, and garnish with fresh mint sprigs and tuile cookies.

> *Note:* The mousse, cake, and ice cream may be made up to 1 day in advance and stored separately. The mousse cakes may be assembled up to 6 hours in advance and refrigerated.

# Chocolate Tuile Cookies

### Richard Leach

GOTHAM BAR AND GRILL
NEW YORK, NEW YORK

**MAKES ABOUT 48 COOKIES**

The chef serves these crispy wafers with his Riot in Chocolate, but they could be the stars themselves with a bowl of ice cream as part of a cookie assortment.

| | | | |
|---|---|---|---|
| ½ | cup (1 stick) unsalted butter at room temperature | 1¼ | cups confectioners' sugar |
| ¼ | cup honey | ¼ | cup unsweetened cocoa |
| ½ | cup all-purpose flour | ¼ | cup egg whites (2 or 3) |

> *To make the cookies:* Preheat the oven to 375°F. In a large bowl combine the butter and honey and beat about 5 minutes until the mixture is smooth and pale in color. Sift the flour, confectioners' sugar, and cocoa together. Add to the butter and honey and mix until incorporated. Slowly add the egg whites and mix until smooth. Use an X-acto blade or a sharp paring knife to make a stencil from the top of a plastic deli or cottage cheese container by cutting out any shape you wish (the chef uses a leaf shape). Place the plastic top on a well-greased jellyroll pan and spread the batter in it until the batter is thin and smooth. Remove the plastic top to leave the shaped batter. Repeat until all the cookies have been made. Bake in the preheated oven for 5 to 6 minutes or until the cookies are firm and dry. Remove from the baking sheet with a large spatula and let cool on waxed paper.

> *Note:* The cookies may also be baked in circles by pouring the batter directly onto the pan, then molded by draping them over a rolling pin, or by laying them over the upturned bottom of a cup to form a basket shape. This must be done immediately after the cookies are taken from the oven, before they cool.

# Chocolate Parfait

### Bruce Molzan
RUGGLES GRILL
HOUSTON, TEXAS

**SERVES 8**

Chocolate cake, layered with chocolate mousse and fresh berries, is drizzled with one or more sauces and garnished with additional berries in this elegant dessert.

## CHOCOLATE CAKE:

| | |
|---|---|
| 2 | tablespoons unsalted butter at room temperature |
| 1¾ | cups plus 2 tablespoons unbleached all-purpose flour |
| 2 | cups sugar |
| ¾ | cup unsweetened cocoa |
| 2 | teaspoons baking soda |
| 1 | teaspoon baking powder |
| 1 | teaspoon salt |
| 1 | cup brewed coffee |
| 1 | cup buttermilk |
| ½ | cup vegetable oil |
| 2 | eggs |
| 1 | teaspoon vanilla extract |

## CHOCOLATE MOUSSE:

| | |
|---|---|
| 11 | ounces semisweet chocolate, chopped |
| 6 | tablespoons unsalted butter, melted |
| 4 | eggs, separated, at room temperature |
| 2 | cups heavy (whipping) cream |
| 2 | tablespoons confectioners' sugar, sifted |
| 1 | teaspoon vanilla extract |

## FOR ASSEMBLY:

| | |
|---|---|
| ¾ | cup Chambord liqueur |
| 2 | cups fresh berries |
| 1 | cup each white and dark chocolate shavings (do not pack down) |

## GARNISH:

| | |
|---|---|
| ½ | cup one or more sauces such as crème anglaise, raspberry, chocolate, or strawberry (page 187) |
| 8 | Chocolate Triangles (recipe follows) |
| ¼ | cup confectioners' sugar, sifted |
| | Additional fresh berries |

✍ *To make chocolate cake:* Preheat the oven to 350°F. Butter a 10-inch round springform pan and lightly dust it with flour. Sift all the dry ingredients together into a large bowl. Add the coffee, buttermilk, and oil, and beat until combined. Continuing to beat, add the eggs then the vanilla. Pour the batter into the prepared pan and bake for 25 to 30 minutes or until a toothpick inserted in the center comes out clean. Remove from the pan and let cool.

✍ *To make the chocolate mousse:* In a double boiler over simmering water, melt the chocolate. Stir in the melted butter. Mix in the egg yolks, stirring constantly to incorporate the yolks and to prevent them from scrambling. Remove from heat and let cool for 10 to 15 minutes. In a large bowl beat the egg whites until stiff, glossy peaks form. Fold the whites into the chocolate while it is still warm. In a deep bowl whip the cream to soft peaks, then blend in the sugar and vanilla. It is important not to overwhip this mixture. Fold the cream into the chocolate mixture and set aside.

☞ *To assemble the parfaits:* Place eight 3x1½ inch pastry rings on a sided baking sheet lined with waxed paper or parchment paper. Cut additional paper into eight 12x4½-inch strips. Fold the strips into thirds lengthwise and place inside the molds to make collars extending 1½ inches above the rings. Using another 3x1½-inch pastry ring, cut 4 circles from the cake, then cut each circle into 2 layers. Place 1 layer in the bottom of each ring. Drizzle each with 1 tablespoon of the Chambord. Arrange 1 layer of berries on top of each cake layer. Dice the remaining cake and place in a bowl. Drizzle with the remaining Chambord and let stand for a few minutes.

Scoop the mousse into the rings over the berries. Top each with some of the diced cake pieces. Sprinkle 1 heaping tablespoonful of white chocolate shavings over each parfait. Repeat with the dark chocolate shavings. Refrigerate for at least 3 hours.

☞ *To serve:* Remove the rings and paper from the parfaits. Drizzle the sauces over and around the plates. Garnish each parfait with 1 chocolate triangle or a purchased wafer. Dust the plates with confectioners' sugar and garnish with the berries.

☞ *Chocolate triangles:* In a double boiler over simmering water, melt 6 ounces chopped bittersweet chocolate. Pour out onto a baking sheet lined with waxed paper and spread thinly with a spatula. Drizzle with the white chocolate, using a toothpick to swirl the white chocolate into the dark. Let cool to harden, then break into triangles by hand.

# Big Island Vintage Surprise

*Jeff Walters*

LA MER, HALEKULANI HOTEL
HONOLULU, OAHU

**SERVES 4**

These beautiful chocolate tortes spill warm ganache when pierced by a fork at the table. Carefully seal the ganache in the center of each mold before baking so that it stays intact until the proper moment.

GANACHE:

4    *ounces bittersweet chocolate, chopped*
9    *tablespoons heavy (whipping) cream*

COOKIE DOUGH:

6    *tablespoons unsalted butter*
½    *cup sugar*
¾    *teaspoon vanilla extract*

⅛    *teaspoon salt*
6    *tablespoons unsweetened cocoa*
¾    *cup plus 2 tablespoons unbleached all-purpose flour*

GARNISH:

*Unsweetened cocoa for dusting*
*Confectioners' sugar for dusting*

✧ *To make the ganache:* Place the chocolate in a small bowl. In a small saucepan bring the cream to scalding. Pour over the chocolate. Stir until the chocolate melts and the mixture is smooth. Let cool to room temperature.

✧ *To make the cookie dough:* In a large bowl combine the butter, sugar, vanilla, and salt and beat just until blended. Do not overbeat. The dough should be moist; if it is too dry, moisten with a little water. Sift the cocoa and flour together on top of the batter and mix slowly until blended.

✧ *To assemble:* Brush the interior of 4 individual soufflé dishes with melted butter and coat with cocoa. Reserve one-fourth of the dough. Divide the remaining dough among the dishes, pressing it into the bottom and sides of the dishes. Tamp down firmly in the center with a dowel, leaving a hollow. Pour the ganache into the hollow to within ¼ inch of the top of the dish. Refrigerate for 30 minutes.

Preheat the oven to 375°F. Cover the ganaches with the reserved dough and seal. Bake for 15 minutes or until set and lightly browned.

✧ *To serve:* Dust 4 dessert plates with cocoa and confectioners' sugar. Unmold the hot cookie shells onto the plates. Be careful not to break the shells. Dust the confectioners' sugar over the tops.

*Chocolate Cake*

*Chocolate Cake with Roasted Banana Sauce*

*A Riot In Chocolate*

*Chocolate Parfait*

*The Unforgettable Torte*

*Chocolate Gourmandise*

*Warm Valrhona Chocolate Cake with Vanilla Ice Cream*

*Chocolate Roulade with Bittersweet Hazelnut Filling*

*Lilikoi Truffle*

# Chocolate Pizza

*John Caluda*
COFFEE COTTAGE
NEW ORLEANS, LOUISIANA

**SERVES 16**

Delicious and witty, John Caluda's version of pizza has a chocolate crust and fruit toppings. The crust portion may be made a day ahead, because it must be cold and firm when used.

CRUST:

| | |
|---|---|
| 2 | *cups (4 sticks) butter at room temperature* |
| 2¼ | *cups sugar* |
| 12 | *eggs* |
| 1 | *cup cocoa* |
| 6 | *ounces unsweetened chocolate, chopped* |

TOPPINGS:

| | |
|---|---|
| 1 | *cup Grand Marnier* |
| ¾ | *cup raspberry jam or sauce* |
| 6 | *peaches, peeled and sliced* |
| 6 | *kiwi, peeled and sliced* |
| 2 | *cups strawberries, hulled* |
| 1 | *cup raspberries or blackberries* |
| 1 | *cup blueberries* |
| 2 | *ounces white chocolate, shaved* |
| 1 | *cup almonds, roasted and chopped* |

&#10148; *To make the crust:* Preheat the oven to 250°F. Coat two 12-inch tortes or layer cake pans with vegetable spray or butter. In the bowl of an electric mixer combine the butter and sugar, and cream with the paddle attachment until the mixture is light and fluffy. Turn the mixer to low speed. In a small bowl beat the eggs with a fork by hand to break them up, then beat into the mixture. Scrape down the sides of the bowl. Turn the mixer to medium speed and sift in the cocoa, scraping the bowl often.

In a small heavy pan over gently simmering water melt the chocolate (alternatively, melt the chocolate in a microwave for 1 minute in most). Gently beat it into the batter. Spread the batter into the pans and bake for 1 hour or until slightly firm. This will not feel like a traditional cake: It will still feel soft, but will firm up when cooled. When cool, remove the cake from the pan, then flip it back over so that it is right side up.

&#10148; *To prepare the toppings:* Place each fruit in a separate small bowl and drizzle with Grand Marnier. Set aside to soak at least 1 hour.

&#10148; *To assemble:* Spread a thin layer of raspberry jam or sauce over the top of the chocolate crust. Spread the peach, kiwi, and strawberry slices from the middle of the pie outward, leaving a ½-inch border. Top with fresh raspberries or blackberries and the soaked blueberries. Sprinkle with white chocolate shavings and sprinkle a circle of crushed almonds around the rim. You can serve it in a cardboard pizza box.

# Chocolate Gourmandise

## Susan Boulot

HEATHMAN HOTEL
PORTLAND, OREGON

**SERVES 6 TO 8**

Individual flourless chocolate cakes baked in ramekins, served warm with chocolate sauce, a chocolate tuile leaf, and a scoop of vanilla ice cream, garnished with gold leaf and a dusting of cocoa on the plate.

CHOCOLATE CAKE:

| | |
|---|---|
| 4 | ounces dark bittersweet chocolate, chopped |
| ½ | cup (1 stick) unsalted butter |
| 3 | whole eggs |
| ½ | cup cocoa |
| 1½ | cups sugar |

CHOCOLATE SAUCE:

| | |
|---|---|
| 1 | cup corn syrup |
| 1 | cup sugar |
| 1¼ | cups water |

| | |
|---|---|
| 1 | cup unsweetened cocoa |
| 1 | pound extra-bitter chocolate, finely chopped |

CHOCOLATE LEAF OR TUILES:

| | |
|---|---|
| 1 | cup confectioners' sugar |
| ½ | cup (1 stick) unsalted butter |
| ½ | cup honey |
| ½ | cup egg whites |
| ½ | cup cocoa |
| 1½ | cups all-purpose flour (may need only 1¼ cups) |

*To prepare the cakes:* Preheat the oven to 275°F. Butter 6 to 8 ramekins (2 inches deep and 2 to 3 inches in diameter).

In a stainless steel bowl or the top of a double boiler combine the chocolate and butter. Place over simmering water and melt together, stirring occasionally.

In the bowl of an electric mixer beat the eggs until lemon-colored and fluffy. They will thicken slightly as beaten, and form a ribbon. Stop the machine, add the cocoa and sugar all at once, and slowly restart the mixer and incorporate the cocoa and sugar, increasing the speed slowly. Stop occasionally to scrape the sides of the bowl. Once mixed, add the melted chocolate mixture and beat at high speed for a few seconds. The batter will thicken as the chocolate is incorporated.

Divide the mixture among the prepared ramekins, filling two-thirds or at most three-fourths full. It is important to leave space in the ramekins, as the cakes will inflate slightly during baking.

Place the ramekins in a baking pan, and add boiling water to a level halfway up the sides of the ramekins. Bake in the preheated oven for 30 to 40 minutes.

Once set, remove from the oven and water bath, and let stand for 10 minutes. Invert the ramekins and remove the cakes. Serve warm.

*Note:* The cakes may be made ahead and reheated in the ramekins in a hot water bath in a preheated oven for 10 to 15 minutes just before serving.

*❧ For the chocolate sauce:* In a heavy saucepan combine the corn syrup, sugar, water, and cocoa, and bring the mixture to a boil, stirring constantly. Once the mixture is smooth, remove the pan from the heat and gradually stir in the chocolate. Stir until melted, smooth, and glossy.

*❧ For the chocolate leaf or tuiles:* In the bowl of an electric mixer combine the sugar and butter and cream together, scraping down the sides of the bowl often. Mix until light and fluffy. Add the honey and mix well. Very slowly begin to incorporate the egg whites, mixing well and allowing the mixture to emulsify before adding more egg whites. This is important, as the batter will separate and appear curdled if the egg whites are added too fast and not allowed to blend into the mixture.

Once the batter is smooth, stop the machine and add the cocoa and flour. Slowly incorporate the dry ingredients into the batter, stopping several times to scrape down the sides of the bowl.

Cut a leaf form out of a 6-inch plastic lid. Use a tree leaf as a design model to trace around. On a silicone sheet on a baking sheet, evenly spread batter in the leaf template. Spread thinly and evenly, but not too thin or the leaves will be brittle once baked.

As an alternative to leaves, the batter may be spread in 3x6-inch strips to form ribbons or flowers, or spread into a 5-inch circle to shape into a cup after baking.

Bake in a 325°F oven for 5 to 7 minutes. The tuiles are done when a slight indentation is left when pressed with a finger. Remove to shape at once.

For cooling, it is helpful to use an empty cardboard egg carton to help in shaping. Place the leaves over the carton to give a gentle natural curve while they cool. Or simply drape over the bottom of a small bowl.

*❧ Note:* If a plain cookie is preferred, simply eliminate the cocoa and add an additional ½ cup of flour to compensate.

*❧ To assemble:* Place one warm chocolate cake off center on a plate. Ladle warm chocolate sauce over and around the cake. If desired, garnish with edible gold leaf. Add a scoop of vanilla ice cream, place a leaf on the plate, and dust the entire plate with cocoa through a sieve.

# The Unforgettable Torte

## Gale E. O'Malley
HILTON HAWAIIAN VILLAGE
HONOLULU, OAHU

**SERVES 4**

This beautiful torte of chocolate cake, hazelnut meringue, and flavored filling is unforgettable, both for its taste and its presentation. The torte could be served by itself, of course. But try the adventure of creating the dramatic chocolate petals and wings; the reward is a piece of art.

### CHOCOLATE GARNISHES:

| | |
|---|---|
| 8 | ounces bittersweet chocolate |
| 8 | striped chocolate wings (page 184) |
| 4 | plain dark chocolate wings (page 184) |
| 8 | 4½-inch plain dark chocolate disks (page 184) |
| 24 | striped chocolate tulip petals (page 184) |

### HAZELNUT MERINGUE:

| | |
|---|---|
| 6 | egg whites |
| ½ | teaspoon cream of tartar |
| 1½ | cups confectioners' sugar, sifted |
| 1 | cup hazelnuts, finely ground |

### CHOCOLATE CAKE:

| | |
|---|---|
| 4 | eggs |
| ⅔ | cup sugar |
| ¼ | cup cocoa |
| | Pinch salt |
| ¾ | cup sifted cake flour |
| 3 | tablespoons unsalted butter, melted |

### WHITE CAKE:

| | |
|---|---|
| 4 | eggs |
| ⅔ | cup sugar |
| 2 | teaspoons vanilla extract |
| | Pinch salt |
| 1 | cup sifted cake flour |
| 3 | tablespoons unsalted butter, melted |

### CHOCOLATE BUTTERCREAM:

| | |
|---|---|
| 3 | ounces bittersweet chocolate, chopped |
| 2 | egg yolks |
| ⅓ | cup sugar |
| ¼ | cup water |
| ½ | cup (1 stick) unsalted butter, at room temperature |

| | |
|---|---|
| ¼ | cup raspberry jam |
| 36 | fresh raspberries |
| 1½ | cups Chocolate Ganache (page 185) |
| ¼ | cup Chambord or other raspberry liqueur |
| 1 | cup heavy (whipping) cream, whipped to soft peaks |
| 1 | tablespoon unsweetened cocoa |
| ½ | pound marzipan |

| | |
|---|---|
| 2 | ounces bittersweet chocolate, melted |
| 1 | tablespoon unsweetened cocoa |
| 4 | lattice dark chocolate leaves (page 183) |

   ✎ *To assemble the chocolate garnishes:* For the wings, line a sheet pan with waxed paper. In the top of a double boiler over simmering water melt 4 ounces of dark chocolate. Lay four striped chocolate wings stripe side up on the waxed paper. Place the melted chocolate in a pastry bag or paper cone with a fine tip and pipe a quarter-size dot of hot chocolate on the lower fourth of each wing. Press a plain chocolate wing onto each dot and hold if necessary until the chocolate sets enough to hold the wing. Pipe another quarter-size dot of hot chocolate onto the lower fourth of the plain wings, and press another striped wing onto each. Place in the refrigerator to set, 5 to 7 minutes.

Line another sheet pan with waxed paper. Place 4 disks on the waxed paper. Pipe a 2-inch dot of hot chocolate on a circle, mounding the dot. Place an assembled wing upright on the dot of chocolate and hold until it sets. Pipe additional hot chocolate at the base of the wing to secure it firmly. Place in the freezer. Repeat with the other wings. The wings can remain in the freezer for up to 2 days.

*To assemble the tulip cups:* Line a sheet pan with waxed paper. In the top of a double boiler over simmering water melt 4 ounces of dark chocolate. Place four disks on the waxed paper. Place the melted chocolate in a pastry bag or paper cone with a fine tip and pipe a 1-inch strip of chocolate on the rim of a disk. With the tips of your fingers lift a striped tulip petal and place it striped side in and point side up into the chocolate. Adjust with a slight outward lean and hold gently until it sets firmly enough to stay. Repeat with five more tulip petals. Place in the freezer. Repeat with the remaining disks and petals. The cups can remain in the freezer for up to 2 days.

*To make the meringues:* Preheat the oven to 200°F. Line a baking pan with parchment paper or heavy brown paper. Trace around a 4-inch ring mold to draw 4 circles on the paper. In a large bowl beat the egg whites and cream of tartar together until foamy. Gradually beat in the confectioners' sugar until the meringue forms stiff peaks. Fold in the ground hazelnuts. Place the meringue in a pastry bag fitted with a medium plain tip and pipe a tight solid spiral on a circle drawn on the prepared baking sheet. Fill in the circle completely. Repeat with the remaining circles and smooth the tops lightly with a spatula or table knife. Bake for 1 hour to 1 hour and 30 minutes or until crisp but not browned. Remove the paper with the meringues and place on a wire rack to cool on the paper.

When cool, lift the meringues from the paper. With a sharp knife trim the edges of each meringue circle to fit inside a 4-inch ring mold. Set aside at room temperature until ready to use.

*To make the chocolate cake:* Preheat the oven to 350°F. Line the bottoms of two 9-inch round cake pans with parchment paper. Warm a deep bowl by filling with warm water, emptying, and drying thoroughly. In the warmed bowl beat the eggs and sugar together until the mixture thickens and a ribbon forms when a spoonful is drizzled on the surface. Fold the cocoa into the egg mixture. Gradually fold the salt and two thirds of the flour into the egg mixture. Blend a large spoonful of the mixture into the butter, then gently fold the butter and the remaining one-third of the flour into the mixture. Pour into the prepared pans and bake for 10 minutes or until a toothpick inserted in the center comes out clean. Let the pan cool for 10 minutes, then remove the cakes from the pans and cool completely on a wire rack. There will be two ½-inch thick cakes.

*To make the white cake:* Preheat the oven to 350°F. Line the bottoms of two 9-inch round cake pans with parchment paper. Warm a deep bowl by filling with warm water, emptying, and drying thoroughly. In the warmed bowl beat the eggs and sugar together until the mixture thickens and a ribbon forms when a spoonful is drizzled on the surface. Stir the vanilla into the egg mixture. Gradually fold two-thirds of the flour and the salt into the egg mixture. Blend a large spoonful of the mixture into the butter, then gently fold the butter and the remaining one-third of the flour into the mixture. Pour into the prepared pans and bake for 10 minutes or until a toothpick inserted in the center comes out clean. Let the pan cool for 10 minutes, then remove the cakes from the pans and cool completely on a wire rack. You will have two ½-inch thick cakes.

     ✑ *To make the buttercream:* In a double boiler over barely simmering water melt the chocolate. Strain the chocolate through a fine-mesh sieve into a small bowl and set aside to cool slightly. In a medium bowl beat the egg yolks until light and fluffy. In a heavy, medium saucepan stir the sugar and water together. Bring to a boil over medium heat, using a pastry brush to brush down any crystals that form on the sides of the pan. Do not stir the mixture while it is heating. Boil to 240°F or until a small amount dropped into a glass of cold water forms a soft, pliable ball. Remove from the heat. While beating the egg yolks on medium speed, gradually pour a thin stream of the sugar mixture into the yolks. Increase the speed to high and continue pouring until all the sugar has been absorbed and the mixture has cooled. It will be light and fluffy.

     In a small, deep bowl cream the butter. Add the butter 1 tablespoon at a time to the mixture, beating constantly, until the butter is incorporated. While beating, gradually pour the chocolate into the buttercream until completely blended and smooth. The buttercream will keep for up to 2 months in the freezer.

     ✑ *To assemble:* Line a baking sheet with parchment paper or aluminum foil. Place four 4-inch ring molds on the sheet. Cut 4 strips of heavy flexible plastic 4 inches wide and 12¾ inches long to fit the inside of the ring molds. Place a plastic strip around the inside of each mold, letting it extend above the top.

     Cut four 4-inch circles from the chocolate cake. Trim each circle to ½ inch thick. Spread a thin layer of raspberry jam on each circle and place one in each prepared mold jam side up. Put the buttercream into a pastry bag fitted with a large plain tip and pipe a layer over each cake. Press 6 of the raspberries into the buttercream of each torte. Put the ganache in a pastry bag fitted with a medium plain tip and pipe a layer of ganache over the raspberries. Reserve the remaining ganache for the final assembly.

     Place a meringue disk over each layer of the ganache, pressing it down slightly. Sprinkle the meringue with Chambord. Press the juice from the remaining 12 raspberries, strain through a fine-mesh sieve, and gently fold the raspberry juice into the whipped cream. Spoon 2 to 3 tablespoons of the raspberry cream over each meringue.

     Cut the white cake into four 4-inch circles. Trim the circles to ½ inch thick and press one on top of the whipped cream in each  mold. Fold the cocoa into the raspberry cream and spoon 2 to 3 tablespoons over each cake. Smooth the tops with the back of a kitchen knife and place the molds in the freezer until firm, 2 to 3 hours.

     Line a baking sheet with parchment or aluminum foil. Place a wire rack on the baking sheet. Roll the marzipan into a ⅛-inch thick sheet and cut four 4-inch circles. In a double boiler over barely simmering water warm the ganache to pouring consistency. Remove the molds from the freezer and gently warm the outsides of the molds with warm towels. Run the tip of a thin, sharp knife around the inside of each mold to loosen the rings. Unmold the tortes onto the wire rack. Strip off the plastic. Press a skewer or fork into each torte and dip completely in the ganache, then place on the rack to drip. Press a marzipan disk onto the top of each torte while the ganache is still soft.

*To serve:* Place a petal cup slightly off center on a dessert plate and carefully center a torte in the cup. Place the melted chocolate in a pastry bag fitted with a small plain tip. Pipe a small pool of melted chocolate on the plate and place a wing garnish in the melted chocolate, holding it in place until the chocolate cools and firms. Dust the top of the marzipan disk with cocoa. Pipe a ½-inch mound of ganache in the center and lean a chocolate lattice leaf against the ganache. Repeat with the remaining tortes.

# Warm Valrhona Chocolate Cakes with Vanilla Ice Cream

*Jean-Georges Vongerichten*
JOJO'S
NEW YORK, NEW YORK

**SERVES 4**

These easy to make cakes are the epitome of chocolate as a comfort food because the centers remain soft, like fudge. People of all ages will adore their taste and texture.

CAKES:

| | |
|---|---|
| 6 | tablespoons unsalted butter |
| 3½ | ounces Valrhona bittersweet chocolate, chopped |
| 2 | eggs |
| 2 | egg yolks |
| ½ | cup sugar |
| 3 | tablespoons all-purpose flour |

GARNISH:

| | |
|---|---|
| | Unsweetened cocoa for dusting |
| 1 | pint finest-quality vanilla ice cream, slightly softened before serving |
| 4 | fresh mint sprigs |

❧ *To make the cakes:* Butter and flour four 4-ounce fluted molds or custard cups and set aside. Preheat the oven to 350°F. Melt the butter and chocolate in a double boiler over barely simmering water, stirring until smooth. Set aside.

In a medium bowl whisk together the eggs and egg yolks. Add the sugar and whisk until foamy. Add the flour and stir to combine. Pour in the chocolate mixture and stir to combine.

Pour the cake batter into the prepared molds. Bake the cakes in the preheated oven for 8 to 10 minutes, or until slightly puffed. Invert the cakes onto 4 individual dessert plates. Dust the cakes with cocoa and place a scoop of softened ice cream to one side of each cake.

❧ *To serve:* Make a cut into the center of the cake to show the texture; the middle of the cakes should be soft and liquid. Garnish with fresh mint sprigs and serve.

❧ *Note:* The cake batter may be placed in the molds up to 2 hours before being baked.

# Lilikoi Truffle

*Mark Hetzel*
THE FOUR SEASONS RESORT MAUI
WAILEA, MAUI

**SERVES 8**

There are two kinds of lilikoi, a light yellow variety and the more intensely colored Tangier variety. In this dessert the light variety is used for the custard and the ganache, and the Tangier variety is used for the garnish. You may, of course, use only one variety in the dessert; it will still taste wonderful.

### LILIKOI CUSTARD:

| | |
|---|---|
| 6 | eggs |
| 1 | cup sugar |
| ¾ | cup Lilikoi Purée (page 187) |
| | Grated zest of 1 orange |
| ½ | cup (1 stick) plus 1 tablespoon unsalted butter |
| 1 | envelope plain gelatin |
| ¼ | cup cold water |
| ¾ | cup heavy (whipping) cream |
| 1 | tablespoon sugar |

### BITTERSWEET CHOCOLATE CAKE:

| | |
|---|---|
| 6 | ounces bittersweet chocolate, chopped |
| 4 | ounces unsweetened chocolate, chopped |
| 1 | cup eavy (2 sticks) unsalted butter, cut up |
| 5 | eggs |
| 4 | egg yolks |
| ½ | cup sugar |

| | |
|---|---|
| 3/4 | cup unbleached all-purpose flour |
| 6 | ounces bittersweet chocolate, chopped |

### LILIKOI GANACHE:

| | |
|---|---|
| 12 | ounces bittersweet chocolate, chopped |
| 9 | ounces milk chocolate, chopped |
| 6 | tablespoons heavy (whipping) cream |
| 4 | tablespoons unsalted butter |
| ¾ | cup sugar |
| ⅔ | cup Lilikoi Purée (page 187) |

### GARNISH:

| | |
|---|---|
| | Unsweetened cocoa powder for dusting |
| 1 | cup Tangier lilikoi juice and seeds |
| 4 | lilikoi, halved lengthwise |
| 24 | lilikoi leaves |

*To make the custard:* In a double boiler over barely simmering water stir together the eggs and sugar and let warm to 100°F.

In a heavy saucepan bring the lilikoi purée, zest, and butter to a boil over medium-high heat.

Meanwhile, sprinkle the gelatin over the cold water and let sit for 3 minutes. Add a large spoonful of the hot purée to the egg mixture and blend, then whisk the egg mixture into the hot purée. Reduce heat to low and cook, stirring constantly for 2 minutes, until the mixture thickens and coats the spoon. Remove from the heat and add the gelatin, stirring until it is completely dissolved. Set the pan in a bowl of ice water and stir until cold.

In a deep bowl whip the cream until it forms soft peaks, adding the sugar gradually as you beat. Fold in the custard, cover with plastic wrap, and refrigerate at least 1 hour or overnight.

❧ *To make the cake:* Preheat the oven to 350°F. Line a jelly roll pan with parchment paper or aluminum foil. In the top of a double boiler set over barely simmering water melt the chocolates and butter, and bring the temperature of the mixture to 100°F. Stir to blend. Set aside.

In a medium bowl whisk the eggs, egg yolks, and sugar until foamy, about 2 minutes. Stir the warm chocolate into the egg mixture, then stir in the flour. Pour into the prepared pan and spread with a spatula to fill the pan evenly. Bake for 10 minutes, or until just firm; do not over-bake.

Let cool to the touch, remove from the pan, and let cool completely. Using a 2½-inch diameter cookie cutter or glass, cut 8 circles from the cake. Cut the remaining cake into ½-inch dice.

❧ *To make the chocolate cups:* In a double boiler over barely simmering water melt the chocolate. Brush eight 2½-inch diameter half-space molds with the chocolate to form a thin shell and put in the freezer to set.

❧ *To make the ganache:* In a large double boiler over barely simmering water melt the chocolates together. In a heavy saucepan stir the cream, butter, sugar, and lilikoi purée together and bring to a boil over medium-high heat. Gradually add the hot cream mixture to the melted chocolate, stirring constantly until smooth and shiny. Remove the pan from the heat and let cool until slightly firm.

❧ *To assemble:* Line a jelly roll pan with a parchment or waxed paper and place a wire rack on top. Fold the diced cake into the custard. Fill the chocolate cup molds with the custard mixture. Place the cake circles over the custard mixture, sealing the chocolate cups. Unmold the chocolate cups, warming the molds slightly with a warm towel to loosen the chocolate, and invert onto the wire rack. With a small spatula or flat knife, spread the ganache over the cups to coat. Allow to set slightly, then touch a spatula or the back of a spoon to the ganache and pull it away, leaving a tiny lifted curl of ganache. Repeat randomly all over each truffle to make each look prickly. Place in the refrigerator to set about 15 minutes.

❧ *To serve:* With a metal spatula lift the truffles and place one on each dessert plate. Dust lightly with cocoa. Spoon 2 tablespoons of lilikoi juice with seeds around each truffle. Place 1 lilikoi half on each plate and garnish with three leaves.

# Cassata Parfait Torte

*Warren LeRuth*

LERUTH'S
NEW ORLEANS, LOUISIANA

**MAKES FOUR 9-INCH CAKES, OR 40 SERVINGS**

CHOCOLATE GENOISE:

| | |
|---|---|
| 7 | eggs |
| 2/3 | cup sugar |
| 1/2 | cup all-purpose flour |
| 3 | tablespoons cornstarch |
| 1/4 | cup cocoa |
| 2 | teaspoons grated lemon rind |

PARFAIT FILLING:

| | |
|---|---|
| 3 | cups heavy (whipping) cream |
| 9 | egg yolks |

| | |
|---|---|
| 3/4 | cup confectioners' sugar |
| 2 | teaspoons vanilla extract |
| 1 | teaspoon grated lemon rind |

ASSEMBLY:

| | |
|---|---|
| 1/4 | cup glacéed (candied) fruit, diced |
| 1/4 | cup maraschino cherries, chopped |
| | Whipped cream |

*To make the chocolate genoise:* Grease and flour two 9-inch cake pans. In a bowl mix the eggs and sugar. Heat over hot water, stirring constantly to 110°F. Remove the pan from the heat and whip with an electric mixer on high speed for 8 to 12 minutes until very light and fluffy. In a medium bowl sift the flour, cornstarch, and cocoa together 3 times. Carefully fold the dry ingredients and lemon rind into the egg mixture. Pour into the prepared cake pans. Bake at 350°F for about 25 to 30 minutes until set and springy. Remove from the oven, invert the cakes onto racks, and cool.

*To make the parfait filling:* In a large bowl whip the cream to stiff peaks and refrigerate until use. In the bowl of an electric mixer whip the egg yolks, sugar, and vanilla on high speed for 7 to 9 minutes until very light. Add the lemon rind. Gently fold the egg yolk mixture into the whipped cream.

*To assemble:* Cut waxed paper into four 9-inch circles and place in the bottoms of four 9-inch cake pans. Spoon the filling evenly into the cake pans, just enough to cover the bottoms. Sprinkle glacéed fruit and cherries on top of the filling. Spoon the remainder of the filling over the fruit. Split both baked cakes horizontally and place one split cake layer on top of the filling in each pan. Freeze overnight. Unmold so that the cake layer will be on the bottom and peel off the waxed paper. Decorate the tops of the cakes with piped whipped cream and whole maraschino cherries. Keep frozen until serving time.

# Chocolate Grand Marnier Cake

*Jean-Luc Albin*

MAURICE'S FRENCH PASTRIES
NEW ORLEANS, LOUISIANA

**SERVES 12**

CHOCOLATE CAKE:

| | |
|---|---|
| 1½ | cups sifted all-purpose flour |
| 2 | tablespoons cocoa |
| 1 | teaspoon baking soda |
| | Pinch salt |
| 1¼ | cups sugar |
| ½ | cup (1 stick) unsalted butter |
| 1 | teaspoon vanilla extract |
| 1 | egg |
| 1 | cup milk |

CHOCOLATE GANACHE:

| | |
|---|---|
| 2 | pounds semisweet chocolate, chopped |

| | |
|---|---|
| 4 | cups heavy (whipping) cream |
| ¼ | cup sugar |
| ½ | cup Grand Marnier or other orange-flavored liqueur |
| ½ | cup strawberry preserves |

GARNISH:

| | |
|---|---|
| 8 | fresh strawberries |
| 4 | ounces semisweet chocolate |
| | Cocoa for dusting |
| | Confectioners' sugar for dusting |

☙ *To make the cake:* Preheat the oven to 350°F. Grease and line two 8-inch cake pans with parchment paper. In a medium bowl combine the flour, cocoa, baking soda, and salt. In the bowl of an electric mixer combine the sugar and butter and cream together until fluffy. Add the vanilla extract. Beat in the egg and continue to beat at medium speed for 3 to 4 minutes. Gradually beat in the blended dry ingredients. With the mixer running, gradually add the milk and beat until smooth. Pour the batter into the prepared pans. Bake for 30 minutes or until a toothpick inserted in the centers comes out clean. Remove from the oven and cool on a wire rack for 30 minutes.

Remove the cakes from the pans, lift off the parchment paper, and let cool completely.

☙ *To make the ganache:* In a medium saucepan combine the chocolate, cream, and sugar. Bring to a boil over medium heat and cook, stirring constantly, until the chocolate is melted and the mixture is smooth. Let cool.

☙ *To serve:* In a small, heavy pan over low heat melt ¼ cup of the ganache. Dip the fresh strawberries in the melted ganache, and set aside on a wire rack to cool.

Sprinkle one cake liberally with Grand Marnier. Spread with the strawberry preserves. Place the remaining ganache in a pastry bag fitted with a large fluted tip and pipe a spiral of ganache on top of the preserves. Top with the second cake. Sprinkle the top with Grand Marnier and pipe ganache over the entire outside of the cake. With a spatula, spread the ganache evenly over the cake. Pour the remaining melted ganache on the top of the cake. Place the cake in the refrigerator to chill.

Shave the remaining four ounces of chocolate: Pull a vegetable parer over the chocolate, or pull the chocolate over the broad cutter of a food grater. Transfer the chilled cake to a serving plate. Pipe a fluted ring of ganache around the bottom of the cake. Arrange the largest shavings in rosettes on top of the cake, pressing them into the ganache covering. Garnish the top with the chocolate-dipped strawberries. Press the remaining shavings around the cake to cover it. Dust with cocoa and confectioners' sugar.

# Chocolate Genoise Truffle Torte with Fresh Berries

*Libby Stritch*

SLIGHTLY NORTH OF BROAD
CHARLESTON, SOUTH CAROLINA

**SERVES 8**

Although the ingredient list and number of techniques may seem formidable, this elegant dessert is actually quite easy to execute.

CHOCOLATE GENOISE:

| | |
|---|---|
| 5 | eggs |
| ¾ | cup sugar |
| ⅓ | cup all-purpose flour |
| ⅓ | cup cocoa |
| 1 | tablespoon butter |
| 1 | tablespoon brandy |

SIMPLE SYRUP:

| | |
|---|---|
| 1 | cup sugar |
| 1 | cup water |

CHOCOLATE TRUFFLE CREAM:

| | |
|---|---|
| 17 | ounces dark chocolate, chopped |
| 1½ | cups heavy (whipping) cream |
| 3 | egg yolks |
| 6 | tablespoons Chambord |

WHITE CHOCOLATE TRUFFLE CREAM:

| | |
|---|---|
| 17 | ounces white chocolate, chopped |
| 1½ | cups heavy (whipping) cream |
| 3 | egg yolks |
| 6 | tablespoons Chambord |

MACERATED RASPBERRIES:

| | |
|---|---|
| ½ | cup sugar |
| | Zest and juice from 2 oranges |
| | Zest and juice from 2 lemons |
| 6 | tablespoons Chambord |
| 3 | pints fresh raspberries |

GARNISH:

| | |
|---|---|
| | Fresh raspberries |
| | White chocolate shavings |
| | Fresh mint |

    *To make the genoise:* Preheat the oven to 350°F. Line the bottom of a greased 10½-inch springform pan with waxed paper, grease the paper, and dust the pan with flour, tapping out the excess. In the large bowl of an electric mixer beat the eggs with the sugar on high speed for 5 minutes or until the mixture is pale yellow and forms a ribbon when the beaters are lifted. In a separate bowl sift the flour and cocoa together. Fold the dry ingredients into the egg mixture until the batter is just combined. In a small saucepan over low heat melt the butter with the brandy. Fold the butter mixture into the batter gently but thoroughly. Pour the batter into the pan, smoothing the top. Bake the cake in the middle of the oven for 20 minutes or until a tester comes out clean. Transfer the cake to a rack and let cool.

    *To make the simple syrup:* In a small, heavy-bottomed saucepan combine the sugar and water and let this mixture come to a slow simmer over medium heat. Cook, stirring occasionally, until a syrup is formed. Remove the pan from the heat.

🕭 *To make the chocolate truffle cream:* In a metal bowl set over a pan of barely simmering water, melt the dark chocolate with 1¼ cups of heavy cream, stirring until the mixture is smooth. Remove the bowl from the heat and let the mixture cool. In the large bowl of an electric mixer combine the egg yolks, Chambord, and ¼ cup of cream and beat on high speed until the mixture is tripled in volume. Fold in the dark chocolate mixture gently but thoroughly.

Brush the genoise with 2 tablespoons of simple syrup. While still in the springform pan, spoon the chocolate truffle cream onto the cake, spreading to cover, until cream is about 1 inch thick. Refrigerate while making the white chocolate truffle cream.

🕭 *To make the white chocolate truffle cream:* In a metal bowl set over a pan of barely simmering water melt the white chocolate with 1¼ cups of heavy cream, stirring until the mixture is smooth. Remove the bowl from the heat and let the mixture cool. In the large bowl of an electric mixer combine the egg yolks, Chambord, and ¼ cup of cream and beat on high speed until the mixture is tripled in volume. Fold in the white chocolate mixture gently but thoroughly.

🕭 *To make the macerated raspberries:* In a clean mixing bowl combine the sugar, orange juice, orange zest, lemon juice, lemon zest, Chambord, and raspberries. Stir until smooth and refrigerate, covered.

🕭 *To assemble:* Remove the cake from the refrigerator and spread the white chocolate truffle cream onto the chocolate truffle cream and smooth with a rubber spatula. The cream should be level with the top of the pan. Refrigerate for at least 30 minutes. Run a sharp knife around the edge and remove the side of the pan. Decorate the finished cake with fresh raspberries and white chocolate shavings.

🕭 *To present:* Place slices of cake on individual serving plates and spoon macerated raspberries on the plates. Garnish with sprigs of fresh mint.

# Chocolate Mousse Cake with Strawberry Sauce

### Bob Roth

THE STEAK KNIFE
NEW ORLEANS, LOUISIANA

**SERVES 8**

The easy-to-put-together chocolate mousse cake may be made a day in advance and frozen, then assembled just before serving.

CHOCOLATE MOUSSE:

| | |
|---|---|
| 8 | ounces semisweet chocolate chips |
| ½ | tablespoon butter |
| 4 | cups heavy (whipping) cream |
| 4 | cups sugar |
| 1 | tablespoon brandy |
| 1 | tablespoon Tia Maria or other coffee liqueur |
| 1 | tablespoon Grand Marnier or other orange liqueur |
| 3 | eggs, separated |

SPONGE CAKE:

| | |
|---|---|
| 8 | eggs |
| 1 | cup sugar |
| 2 | tablespoons cornstarch |

| | |
|---|---|
| 1¼ | cups all-purpose flour |
| 5 | tablespoons butter, melted and at room temperature |
| 1 | teaspoon pure vanilla extract |

STRAWBERRY SAUCE:

| | |
|---|---|
| 4 | cups strawberries, hulled |
| 1 | tablespoon strawberry liqueur (optional) |
| 3 | tablespoons honey |
| ½ | cup dry white wine |
| 1 | cup heavy (whipping) cream |
| 1 | tablespoon Grand Marnier or other orange liqueur |
| 1 | pint fresh strawberries for garnish |

❧ *To make the chocolate mousse:* In a double boiler over barely simmering water melt the chocolate and butter, stirring until smooth. Set aside to cool slightly. In a deep bowl whip the cream until soft peaks form. Add the sugar, then add the brandy and liqueurs. Blend thoroughly. Mix a small amount of the whipped cream into the melted chocolate, then fold that mixture back into the whipped cream.

In a double boiler over barely simmering water whisk the egg yolks for 2 minutes. Set aside. In a large bowl beat the egg whites until soft peaks form. Fold the egg yolks, then the beaten whites into the chocolate whipped cream until smooth and blended. Cover and refrigerate.

❧ *To make the cake:* Preheat the oven to 350°F. Grease and dust with flour a 4x12-inch pan. In a double boiler over barely simmering water mix together the eggs and sugar and beat about 4 to 5 minutes until thickened and smooth. Set aside. Sift the cornstarch and flour together and fold into the egg mixture. Fold the butter and vanilla extract into the batter. Pour into the prepared pan. Bake for 30 to 40 minutes or until the cake springs back when pressed. Let cool.

Cut the cooled cake into 6 slices to fit a loaf pan. Line a cake pan with the slices of sponge cake. Ladle in the chilled chocolate mousse until the pan is full. Cover the mousse with slices of sponge cake. Cover with plastic wrap and freeze.

*To make the sauce:* In a blender or food processor purée the berries. Strain through a fine-mesh sieve. In a medium saucepan heat the purée over low heat and stir in the remaining ingredients. Let cool, then cover and refrigerate.

*To make the flavored whipped cream:* In a small, deep bowl whip the cream until soft peaks form. Fold in the orange liqueur. Cover and refrigerate.

*To serve:* Warm a large knife in hot water and cut the mousse cake into 8 slices. Ladle strawberry sauce onto each of eight serving plates. Place a slice of frozen mousse on the sauce. Place in the refrigerator until semisoft. Top with flavored whipped cream, garnish with strawberries, and serve.

# Marquise au Chocolat

Gerard Thabuis
LA SAVOIE
NEW ORLEANS, LOUISIANA

**SERVES 8**

## CHOCOLATE SPONGE CAKE:

1     cup plus 3 tablespoons all-purpose flour
½     cup cocoa
¼     cup cornstarch
½     teaspoon baking soda
10    eggs
10    egg yolks
1     cup oil
¾     cup plus 2 tablespoons sugar

## CHOCOLATE CREAM FILLING:

5     ounces semisweet baking chocolate
6     tablespoons strong black coffee
7     egg yolks
1     cup sugar
1¼    cups butter, melted

¾     cup cocoa
2     cups heavy (whipping) cream
¼     cup confectioners' sugar

## GRAND MARNIER SAUCE:

1     cup heavy (whipping) cream
1     cup sugar
      Grated rind from 1 orange
1     cup orange juice
½     cup Grand Marnier
      Few drops yellow food coloring

## ASSEMBLY:

4     cups strong coffee
      Grand Marnier Sauce

ە To make the sponge cake: Preheat the oven to 325°F. In a medium bowl sift together the flour, cocoa, cornstarch, and baking soda. In the top of a double boiler over simmering water whip the eggs, egg yolks, oil, and sugar with a mixer at high speed until the mixture is pale yellow and forms a ribbon. Remove from the heat and slowly add the dry ingredients. Pour the batter into a well-buttered 10x15-inch cake pan. Bake for 40 minutes.

Remove from the oven and cool in the pan for 5 minutes. Remove the cake from the pan and allow to cool thoroughly on a rack.

ە To make the chocolate cream filling: In a pan set over almost simmering water stir the semisweet chocolate and coffee until the chocolate is melted and smooth. Set aside to cool. In a medium bowl combine the yolks and sugar and whip until the mixture becomes a glossy, pale yellow. Add the chocolate and coffee mixture. In another bowl mix the melted butter and cocoa, then fold into the chocolate and egg yolk mixture. In a separate bowl whip the cream to soft peaks. Add the confectioners' sugar and whip to stiff peaks. Fold the whipped cream carefully into the chocolate mixture. Reserve.

✍ *To make the Grand Marnier sauce:* In a large bowl combine the cream, sugar, orange rind, orange juice, Grand Marnier, and a few drops of yellow food coloring. Mix well. Reserve.

✍ *To assemble:* Slice the sponge cake into $\frac{1}{2}$-inch thick strips and brush with the coffee. Line the bottom and sides of a 5x9-inch loaf pan with waxed paper cut to fit. Cover the bottom and sides of the pan with the strips of cake. Spoon the chocolate cream filling over the cake strips. Cover the top with more coffee-soaked cake strips. Cover with aluminum foil and place a 1-pound weight on the top. Refrigerate overnight. Remove the aluminum foil and invert the dessert onto a serving platter to unmold.

✍ *To serve:* Pour the Grand Marnier sauce on the bottom of the serving plates and place the sliced marquise on top.

# Chocolate-Rum Truffle Cake

*Richard Rivera*

AMBROSIA EURO-AMERICAN PÂTISSERIE
BARRINGTON, ILLINOIS

**SERVES 10**

A host of popular flavors—almond, vanilla, and raspberry, along with chocolate and rum-take on a variety of roles in this big production number. This dessert is almost a course in the art of pastry making. The bisquit décor is similar to a roulade; meringue is folded into the batter so that it is flexible after baking.

## BISQUIT DÉCOR SHEET:

| | |
|---|---|
| 6 | egg yolks |
| 1 | whole egg |
| 1 | cup plus 2 tablespoons sugar |
| 2 | teaspoons almond extract or vanilla extract |
| 1 | cup cake flour, sifted |
| ¾ | cup egg whites (about 6 whites) |
| 3 | tablespoons unsweetened cocoa |

## GENOISE:

| | |
|---|---|
| 3 | large eggs |
| 6 | tablespoons sugar |
| ½ | cup cake flour |
| ½ | teaspoon baking powder |
| 2 | teaspoons vanilla extract |
| 1 | tablespoon unsalted butter, melted |

## RUM SYRUP:

| | |
|---|---|
| 2 | cups water |
| 1 | cup sugar |
| ¼ | cup Myer's dark rum, or to taste |

## CHOCOLATE BAVARIAN CREAM:

| | |
|---|---|
| 12 | ounces semisweet chocolate, chopped |
| ¼ | cup water |
| 2 | envelopes plain gelatin |
| 1 | cup Crème Anglaise (page 189) |
| 3 | cups heavy (whipping) cream |

## CHOCOLATE GANACHE:

| | |
|---|---|
| 12 | ounces semisweet chocolate, chopped |
| 1 | cup heavy (whipping) cream |

## CHOCOLATE RUM TRUFFLES:

| | |
|---|---|
| 15 | ounces semisweet chocolate, chopped |
| ½ | cup heavy (whipping) cream |
| 1½ | tablespoons unsalted butter |
| 3 | tablespoons sugar |
| 3 | tablespoons Myer's dark rum, to taste |
| 1 | cup unsweetened cocoa |

## MOCHA BUTTERCREAM:

| | |
|---|---|
| 3 | tablespoons water |
| 1 | cup sugar |
| 6 | large egg yolks |
| 2 | cups (4 sticks) unsalted butter at room temperature, cut into small pieces |
| 2 | tablespoons coffee extract or double strength brewed espresso |

## GARNISH:

| | |
|---|---|
| 1¼ | cups apricot jam |
| 1½ | cups Crème Anglaise (page 189) |
| 6 | tablespoons Raspberry Sauce (page 187) |
| | Unhulled fresh strawberries, halved |
| | Fresh raspberries |

 To make the bisquit décor: Preheat the oven to 400°F. Line a 13x7 inch sided baking pan with parchment paper or waxed paper. In the bowl of an electric mixer combine the egg yolks, egg, and 1 cup sugar. Beat at high speed about 10 minutes until the mixture is pale in color and thick. Add the extract. Fold the flour into the egg mixture.

In a large bowl beat the egg whites with 2 tablespoons of sugar until stiff, glossy peaks form. Remove one-third of the batter to a separate bowl and fold the cocoa into it. Refrigerate the remaining batter. Place the chocolate batter in a pastry bag fitted with a plain tip and pipe diagonal stripes onto the prepared pan. The strips should be ½ to ¾ inch thick and spaced 1 inch apart. Place in the freezer until firm to the touch.

Carefully spread the reserved batter over the chocolate. Smooth lightly, so the darker lines are not disturbed. Place in the oven and bake about 10 minutes until golden. Let cool slightly, then remove from the pan. Trim the edges to square them off, then cut into 1-inch wide lengthwise strips. Set aside.

 To make the genoise: Preheat the oven to 350°F. Butter an 8-inch round cake pan and line it with parchment paper or waxed paper. In the bowl of an electric mixer combine the eggs and sugar. Whisk together over simmering water until warm to the touch. Remove and beat with an electric mixer for about 10 minutes until the mixture cools. The mixture will double in volume. In a separate bowl sift together the flour and baking powder. Gently fold the dry ingredients into the egg mixture, then add the vanilla. Fold the butter into the batter and pour into the prepared pan.

Bake for 10 to 15 minutes or until a toothpick inserted in the center comes out clean. Let the cake cool for a few minutes, then remove from the pan. Let the cake cool completely. Using a sharp serrated knife, cut the browned outside surface from the top, bottom, and sides of the cake. Carefully split the cake into 3 layers. Set aside.

 To make the chocolate Bavarian cream: In a double boiler over simmering water melt the chocolate. Place the water in a cup and sprinkle the gelatin over. Let sit for 2 minutes. In a small saucepan combine the crème anglaise and gelatin mixture and heat over low heat until the gelatin dissolves. Stir the crème mixture into the melted chocolate. Let cool to lukewarm. In a deep bowl whip the cream until stiff peaks form, then fold it into the chocolate. Let sit until ready to use.

 To make the chocolate ganache: In a double boiler over simmering water melt the chocolate. In a small saucepan bring the cream to a boil over medium heat. Stir the warm cream into the chocolate, being careful not to beat air into the mixture. Reserve 1 cup for the top of the torte and keep warm. Refrigerate the remaining ganache.

 To make the chocolate-rum truffles: In a double boiler over simmering water melt 9 ounces of the chocolate. In a small saucepan combine the cream, butter, and sugar and heat over low heat until the butter and sugar are melted. Pour the cream mixture into the chocolate and stir until mixed. Let cool slightly, then stir in the rum. Refrigerate until firm.

In a double boiler over simmering water, melt the remaining 6 ounces of the chocolate. Place the cocoa in a pie tin. Roll the chilled truffle mixture into 1-inch balls and place them on the prepared pan lined with parchment paper. You will have 24 to 30 truffles. Refrigerate again for a few minutes. Dip each ball into melted chocolate to coat, then drop the ball into the cocoa and coat it by shaking the container. Transfer to the prepared pan and repeat until all balls are coated. Refrigerate until needed.

*To prepare the mocha buttercream:* In a small saucepan combine the water and sugar and cook over medium heat until the syrup is light and golden and registers 242°F on a candy thermometer or reaches the soft ball stage, when a small amount of the syrup dropped into cold water will form a soft and pliable ball. Let cool slightly.

Place the egg yolks in the bowl of an electric mixer and begin to beat at high speed. Gradually add the sugar syrup and continue to beat until the mixture cools. Gradually add the butter, beating after each addition and stopping occasionally to scrape down the sides of the bowl. Add the coffee extract or espresso.

*To assemble the torte:* Line a baking sheet with parchment paper or waxed paper. Place an 8-inch stainless steel ring that is 3 inches deep on the prepared pan. Place 1 layer of the genoise in the bottom of the ring. Line the sides with the bisquit décor, placing it in the ring with the chocolate-striped side facing the sides. Be sure to press the sections together tightly. Brush the sides and bottom generously with the rum syrup.

Whip the chilled ganache in an electric mixer until creamy, then place it in a pastry bag with a plain tip. Spread a layer of chocolate Bavarian cream over the genoise. Pipe a layer of the ganache on top of the cream. Add a second layer of genoise and gently press down on it to bond. Brush the genoise with rum syrup, then repeat the layers of chocolate Bavarian cream and ganache. Place the last layer of genoise on top and again press down gently. Brush the top with rum syrup and place the cake in the freezer until firm.

Remove the cake from the freezer and wrap a hot towel around the ring for a few seconds to help unmold it. Invert the cake onto the center of a cardboard cake round (preferably gold). Remove the ring. Spread a thin layer of buttercream over the top to seal the porous pastry. Smooth with a wet knife, removing excess. Chill again until the buttercream is firm.

In a small heavy pan warm the jam over low heat. Push the jam through a fine-mesh sieve with the back of a large spoon. Using a pastry brush, coat the sides of the torte with the apricot glaze to seal the sponge. This will retain moisture and give a beautiful sheen. Remove any excess glaze from around the edge of the torte.

The reserved unrefrigerated ganache should now be warm enough to spread, but not so hot that it will melt the buttercream. Ladle the ganache onto the center top of the cake and smooth it outward without going over the edge onto the sides. It should just cover the top. Wipe off any drips from the sides. While the ganache is still warm, space 10 truffles around the outer edge. Refrigerate the cake.

*To serve:* Use a warm knife to cut the cake. Be sure to clean off the knife after each cut to assure attractive servings. Place 1 wedge on each dessert plate. Ladle 2 tablespoons of crème anglaise alongside each portion. Dot the cream in 5 or 6 places with the raspberry sauce and use the point of a knife to pull downward through each dot, making hearts. Brush the strawberries with some of the apricot glaze and garnish the plates with the strawberries and raspberries.

# Macaroon Mocha Buttercream Cake

### Michael Foley
PRINTER'S ROW
CHICAGO, ILLINOIS

**SERVES 8 TO 10**

CHOCOLATE GENOISE:

| | |
|---|---|
| 1 | heaping tablespoon cocoa |
| ¾ | cup plus 2 tablespoons cake flour |
| 6 | eggs |
| ½ | cup plus 2 tablespoons sugar |
| 2 | tablespoons unsalted butter, melted |
| | Zest of 1 orange, grated |

MOCHA BUTTERCREAM:

| | |
|---|---|
| 6 | eggs |
| 1¼ | cups sugar |
| ¼ | cup espresso (strong coffee may be substituted) |
| 8 | ounces unsweetened chocolate, melted |
| 14 | tablespoons (1¾ sticks) room temperature butter, cut into 1-inch cubes |

SYRUP:

| | |
|---|---|
| ¼ | cup water |
| 2 | tablespoons sugar |
| 2 | drops orange liqueur |

GANACHE:

| | |
|---|---|
| 6 | ounces semisweet chocolate |
| 6 | ounces unsweetened chocolate |

ASSEMBLY:

| | |
|---|---|
| 1 | cup ground chocolate macaroons |
| 2 | blood oranges |
| | Mint leaves |

To make the chocolate genoise: Preheat the oven to 350°F. Butter and flour a 6-inch spring-form pan. In a medium bowl sift together the cocoa and cake flour. Break the eggs into a separate mixing bowl and add the sugar. Whisk over warm water just until warm. Then whip with a mixer at high speed until cool, light in consistency, and almost doubled in volume. Fold in the dry ingredients, then the butter and orange zest. Pour the batter into the prepared pan. Bake for about 30 minutes. When cool, cut into 3 layers.

To make the mocha buttercream: In the top of a double boiler whisk together the eggs and sugar over simmering water until the mixture becomes fluffy and triples in volume (bubbles will disappear and it will become a thick cream). Remove from the heat and add the espresso and melted chocolate. Whip with a mixer at high speed for about 7 to 10 minutes until cooled. Gradually add the butter and whip for 3 to 4 minutes until the butter is incorporated. Reserve at room temperature.

To make the syrup: In a small saucepan bring the water and sugar to a boil. Remove the pan from the heat and add the orange liqueur. Reserve at room temperature.

✿ *To make the ganache:* In the top of a double boiler combine the chocolates and slowly melt over warm water. If the mixture seems too thick, add 1 tablespoon of water. Reserve at room temperature.

✿ *To assemble:* In a 6-inch springform pan place 1 layer of chocolate genoise. Baste the cake with half of the syrup. Pipe a layer of buttercream onto the cake. Sprinkle with ground chocolate macaroon. Press down on the layers. Repeat with another layer of genoise, the remaining syrup, buttercream, and ground macaroons. Top with the third layer of genoise. Spread ganache on top. Refrigerate overnight. Unmold and, if desired, pipe additional buttercream on the top and spread on the sides of the cake. To garnish, press additional ground macaroons onto the sides. Let stand until room temperature. Serve with blood orange sections and mint leaves.

# Progrès with Two Chocolate Mousses

*Pierre Pollin*

LE TITI DE PARIS
CHICAGO, ILLINOIS

**SERVES 8 TO 10**

## PROGRÈS LAYER:

| | |
|---|---|
| 3 | *ounces almonds* |
| 1 | *tablespoon plus 1 teaspoon all-purpose flour* |
| 1 | *cup sugar* |
| 3 | *egg whites* |

## DARK CHOCOLATE MOUSSE:

| | |
|---|---|
| 7 | *ounces bittersweet chocolate, chopped (slightly sweetened chocolate available in specialty stores)* |
| 1¾ | *cups heavy (whipping) cream* |

## WHITE CHOCOLATE MOUSSE:

| | |
|---|---|
| 9 | *ounces good-quality white chocolate, chopped* |
| 1½ | *cups heavy (whipping) cream* |

## CRÈME ANGLAISE WITH GRAND MARNIER:

| | |
|---|---|
| 6 | *egg yolks* |
| ½ | *cup plus 1 tablespoon sugar* |
| 2 | *tablespoons Grand Marnier* |
| 2 | *cups plus 2 tablespoons milk* |

## ASSEMBLY:

| | |
|---|---|
| 3 | *ounces white chocolate shavings* |
| 3 | *ounces bittersweet chocolate shavings* |

*To prepare the progrès layer:* Spread the almonds on a baking sheet and toast in a 350°F oven for 5 to 10 minutes, watching carefully to avoid burning. Cool at room temperature. In a food processor blend the almonds with the flour until a powder forms.

Combine the almond powder and ¾ cup of sugar. Set aside. Beat the egg whites to soft peaks. Slowly add the remaining sugar and beat until stiff peaks are formed. Carefully fold the dry ingredients into the egg whites. Pour the batter into an 11-inch springform pan lined with parchment paper. Bake at 350°F for 15 minutes. Let cool completely.

*To make the dark chocolate mousse:* In a heavy saucepan melt the chocolate with half of the whipping cream. Let cool. Whip the remaining cream until stiff and fold into the cooled chocolate. Spread the dark chocolate mousse on the progrès layer. Refrigerate about 30 minutes while preparing the white chocolate mousse.

*To prepare the white chocolate mousse:* In a heavy saucepan melt the chocolate with 1 cup plus 2 tablespoons of the whipping cream. Cool to room temperature. Beat the remaining cream until stiff. Carefully fold into the cooled chocolate. Spread on top of the dark chocolate mousse and return the cake to the refrigerator for several hours or overnight.

☙ *To make the crème anglaise:* In the top of a double boiler over simmering water heat the egg yolks, sugar, and Grand Marnier. In a separate saucepan scald the milk and add to the egg yolk mixture, whisking constantly. Cook over simmering water until the mixture coats a spoon. Cool before serving.

☙ *To assemble:* Unmold the cake and garnish the top with white and bittersweet chocolate shavings just before serving. Serve with crème anglaise.

# Progrès with Grand Marnier

*Roberto Gerometta*
CHEZ MICHEL
SAN FRANCISCO, CALIFORNIA

**SERVES 12**

BISCUIT NOISETTE:

6      egg whites
       Small pinch salt
2      tablespoons lemon juice
2      tablespoons sugar
2      tablespoons to ¼ cup all-purpose flour
5      ounces hazelnuts, finely ground
⅔      cup sugar

SYRUP GRAND MARNIER:

½      cup water
½      cup sugar
1      ounce Grand Marnier

BUTTERCREAM:

2      cups milk
10     egg yolks
1⅓     cups sugar
3¼     cups butter

CRÈME NOISETTE:

1      ounce hazelnut paste or almond paste
1      teaspoon Kirsch
¼      of the Buttercream

MOUSSE:

2      cups heavy (whipping) cream
4      egg yolks
½      to ¾ cup Syrup Grand Marnier
4      ounces semisweet chocolate, melted

CHOCOLATE CREAM:

12     ounces semisweet chocolate
       Remaining Buttercream

GARNISH:

       Sugar
       Flowers

*To make the biscuit noisette:* In a blender combine the egg whites, salt, and lemon juice. Add 1 ounce of sugar to the egg whites while blending. In a large bowl blend the flour, 5 ounces of sugar, and ground hazelnuts. Add the beaten egg whites to the hazelnut-sugar mixture and fold in with a spatula.

Butter the bottom of a baking sheet, and cover with buttered parchment paper. Pour the biscuit dough on the parchment. Bake in a 500°F oven for 5 minutes, turning often. When cooked, cool in the refrigerator.

*To make the syrup Grand Marnier:* In a small saucepan bring the water and sugar to a boil. Remove the pan from the heat and cool in the refrigerator. Add the Grand Marnier to the cooled syrup and reserve. (Note: Three-fourths of this syrup-Grand Marnier mixture will be used in the mousse; the remainder will be used to bunch the various layers of the Progrès.)

✍ *To make the buttercream:* In a saucepan heat the milk. In a bowl whisk together the egg yolks and sugar. Add the heated milk to the egg mixture and whisk off the heat. Return the mixture to the saucepan and whisk while heating until smooth and fairly thick. Remove from the heat and strain back into a bowl. Cool in the refrigerator.

When chilled, remove from the refrigerator and place in a blender. While blending on low speed, add the butter a little at a time. Blend until smooth, then return to the refrigerator.

✍ *To make the crème noisette:* In a bowl combine the hazelnut paste and Kirsch, and mix well with a spatula. Add 4 ounces of buttercream and blend well. Refrigerate for 5 minutes.

✍ *To make the mousse:* In a large bowl whip the cream with whisk. In another bowl over hot water whisk the egg yolks and syrup. Add the melted chocolate to the whipped cream and whisk until smooth. Fold the egg mixture into the chocolate mixture and mix with a spatula.

✍ *To make the chocolate cream:* In a saucepan melt the chocolate, then cool. Add half of the chocolate to the buttercream. Mix well, then add the remaining chocolate (must be done in steps or the cream will break). Refrigerate.

✍ *To assemble:* Remove the biscuit from the refrigerator and cut two circles to the shape of a 10-inch mold. Place the bottom biscuit into the mold and brush with syrup. Spread a layer of crème noisette on top of the syrup. Refrigerate for 2 minutes. Add a layer of mousse, then place the top biscuit on the mousse. Brush with syrup again, then spread with a layer of chocolate cream. Freeze for 5 to 30 minutes. Pipe a layer of chocolate cream on top. Unmold and serve on a tray with a garnish of sugar and real flowers.

# Tarte au Chocolat

Bernard Cretier
LE VICHYSSOIS
CHICAGO, ILLINOIS

**SERVES 8 TO 10**

CAKE:

3⅓ ounces orange chocolate (semisweet chocolate may be substituted)
6 tablespoons plus 2 teaspoons butter
¼ cup plus 2 teaspoons all-purpose flour
⅔ cup sugar
3 eggs

CRANBERRY SAUCE:

1 cup orange juice
½ cup water
6 ounces whole fresh cranberries
½ cup sugar
Zest of ½ orange, grated

FROSTING:

1½ ounces orange chocolate (bittersweet chocolate may be substituted)
1½ ounces bittersweet chocolate (slightly sweetened chocolate may be found in specialty stores)
2 teaspoons butter
6 tablespoons plus 2 teaspoons heavy (whipping) cream

*To make the cake:* Preheat the oven to 375°F. Butter and flour an 8-inch round cake pan. In the top of a double boiler over simmering water melt chocolate. Add the butter, whisking to melt and incorporate. In a separate bowl beat the flour, sugar, and eggs with an electric mixer for about 3 minutes until smooth and creamy. Add the melted chocolate and butter. Pour into the prepared pan. Bake for 20 minutes or until a toothpick inserted in the center comes out clean. Let cool completely before frosting.

*To make the cranberry sauce:* In a saucepan combine the orange juice, water, cranberries, sugar, and orange zest, and boil for 20 minutes, stirring occasionally. Transfer to a food processor and purée. Strain and refrigerate.

*To make the frosting:* In the top of a double boiler melt the chocolate. Add the butter. In a separate saucepan bring the cream to a boil, and add it to the chocolate. Let cool until thick and creamy. Allow to cool.

Spread the frosting over the top and sides of the cake. To garnish, sprinkle the top with cocoa sugar. To serve, pour cranberry sauce around each slice.

# Night and Day Cake

Roland Liccioni
LE FRANCAIS
CHICAGO, ILLINOIS

**SERVES 10 TO 12**

## CHOCOLATE CAKE:

| | |
|---|---|
| 2 | *tablespoons cornstarch* |
| 3 | *tablespoons cake flour* |
| 3 | *tablespoons cocoa* |
| 5 | *eggs, separated* |
| | *Few drops lemon juice* |
| ½ | *cup sugar* |

## GANACHE:

| | |
|---|---|
| 8 | *ounces semisweet chocolate* |
| 2 | *tablespoons butter, softened* |

## SYRUP:

| | |
|---|---|
| ¼ | *cup sugar* |
| ¼ | *cup water* |
| 1 | *ounce dark rum or Grand Marnier* |

## WHITE CHOCOLATE MOUSSE:

| | |
|---|---|
| ½ | *cup plus 1 tablespoon sugar* |
| ¼ | *cup water* |
| 2 | *egg yolks* |
| 1 | *whole egg* |
| 1 | *teaspoon sugar* |
| 2 | *tablespoons dark rum* |
| 1 | *tablespoon Grand Marnier* |
| 1 | *envelope (¼ ounce) unflavored gelatin, dissolved in ¼ cup cold water* |
| 2½ | *ounces white chocolate, melted in a double boiler over warm water* |
| 1¼ | *cups heavy (whipping) cream* |

## ASSEMBLY:

| | |
|---|---|
| 2 | *tablespoons white raisins, halved and soaked in dark rum* |

✍ *To make the chocolate cake:* Preheat the oven to 350°F. Butter and flour a 10-inch round cake pan. In a medium bowl sift together the cornstarch, cake flour, and cocoa. Set aside. In the bowl of an electric mixer beat the egg whites and lemon juice at high speed to soft peaks. Add the sugar and continue to beat until stiff peaks form. Slightly beat the egg yolks and manually fold into the whites. Gradually fold in the dry ingredients, being careful not to deflate the egg whites. Pour the batter into the prepared pan. Bake for 30 minutes or until the sides of the cake pull away from the pan.

✍ *To make the ganache:* In the top of a double boiler melt the chocolate over warm water. Whisk in the butter. Reserve.

✍ *To make the syrup:* In a small saucepan bring the sugar and water to a boil. Remove from the heat and cool. Add the liquor. The syrup will keep indefinitely in a covered jar in the refrigerator.

*To make the white chocolate mousse:* In a small pan combine ½ cup plus 1 tablespoon of sugar and ¼ cup of water and cook to 248°F (the hard ball stage). In a round-bottomed mixing bowl combine the egg yolks, egg, 1 teaspoon of sugar, 1 tablespoon of dark rum, and 1 tablespoon of Grand Marnier. On the stove, set the mixing bowl over a pan of warm water (160°F to 170°F) and constantly beat the mixture until it is warm and foamy. Add the dissolved gelatin; whisk to incorporate. Remove from the heat and, using a mixer set at slow speed, gradually add the sugar water (cooked to the hard ball stage). Continue to mix at slow speed until the mixture is completely cool. Then add the melted white chocolate. In another bowl whip the cream to stiff peaks. Add some to the chocolate mixture; fold in the remainder. Add 1 tablespoon of dark rum for flavor. To avoid loss of volume, use as soon as possible.

*To assemble:* Line a 10-inch round pan with plastic wrap. Slice the cake into 2 layers. Spread half the ganache on one of the layers. Invert the layer into the prepared pan (so the ganache is on the bottom). Brush the layer of cake with half of the syrup. Then sprinkle with rum-soaked raisins and top with the white chocolate mousse. Place the other layer of cake in the mold and brush it with the remaining syrup. Spread ganache on top and refrigerate 6 hours to overnight. Invert and unmold the cake onto a serving plate. Decorate as desired and serve.

*Chocolate Rum Truffle Torte*

*Chocolate-Macadamia Nut Toffee Torte*

*President's Cake*

*Mocha Framboise*

*Flourless Macadamia Nut-Chocolate Cake*

*Chocolate Lover's Cake*

*Gateau Chocolat Fondant*

*Chocolate Mousse Cheesecake*

*Chocolate Tart*

*Frozen Soufflés under a Chocolate Dome*

# Ibarra Chocolate Cake

*Mark Miller*

COYOTE CAFE
SANTA FE, NEW MEXICO

**SERVES 10 TO 12**

CAKE:

| | |
|---|---|
| 2 | cups unblanched almonds |
| 3 | oranges |
| 3 | ounces bittersweet chocolate, grated |
| 1½ | teaspoons ground cinnamon |
| 6 | eggs, separated and at room temperature |
| ½ | cup sugar |

| | |
|---|---|
| 3 | tablespoons freshly squeezed orange juice |
| 3 | tablespoons Grand Marnier |

GLAZE:

| | |
|---|---|
| 5 | ounces bittersweet chocolate |
| ½ | ounce unsweetened chocolate |
| 1 | tablespoon light corn syrup |
| ¾ | cup (1½ sticks) unsalted butter |

ﾒ *To prepare the cake:* Preheat the oven to 350°F. Butter the bottom and sides of a 9-inch springform pan, line with parchment paper, and butter and flour the parchment paper. Roast the almonds on a baking sheet for 5 to 7 minutes or until lightly browned. Place them in a blender or a food processor fitted with a steel blade and grind finely. While the almonds are roasting, remove the orange zest from the oranges with a zester or vegetable peeler and chop finely.

In a small bowl combine the almonds, orange zest, grated chocolate, and cinnamon. Set aside. In a large bowl beat the egg yolks until light and lemon-colored, incorporating as much air as possible. When thick, add the sugar in two parts. In another bowl beat the egg whites until stiff. Beat the dry ingredients, orange juice, and one-third of the egg whites into the egg yolks, then rapidly fold in the remaining egg whites. Pour the batter into the prepared pan and bake in the middle of the preheated oven for 35 to 40 minutes or until the cake pulls away from the sides of the pan.

Loosen the sides of the pan and cool for 10 minutes. Invert the cake onto a rack to cool and remove the paper. When cool, paint with Grand Marnier.

ﾒ *To make the glaze:* Break the chocolate into small pieces. In the top of a double boiler combine the chocolate, corn syrup, and butter. Heat the pan, and turn off the heat as the water comes to a boil. Beat with a whisk until smooth.

Place the cake on a rack over a pan or waxed paper and pour the glaze in the center. Tilt the cake to distribute the glaze evenly, and allow the cake to sit for 45 minutes before serving.

ﾒ *Note:* The cake can be made up to a day in advance and should be kept at room temperature.

# Chocolate Macadamia Nut–Toffee Torte

*Rodney Weddle*

THE DINING ROOM, THE RITZ-CARLTON KAPALUA
KAPALUA, MAUI

**SERVES 8**

Begin in the hardware store: Chef Weddle uses a metal mesh screen door insert as a stencil for his genoise, a squeegee designed for cement work as the perfect scraper for the stencil, and ordinary PVC pipe cut into rings for molds. Look for heavy flexible plastic that is sold in rolls, a masonry comb, and wood-grained paint rollers; they are all tools for the imaginative chef. This torte uses nearly every pastry-making skill, but it can be simplified by eliminating the patterned design on the cake and by using fresh fruit alone for garnish.

### PÂTÉ CIGARETTE:

| | |
|---|---|
| 2 | cups (4 sticks) unsalted butter at room temperature |
| 4 | cups (1 pound) confectioners' sugar, sifted |
| 16 | egg whites |
| 3¼ | cups unbleached all-purpose flour |
| | Dash vanilla extract |
| ⅔ | cup unsweetened cocoa |

### SABLÉ COOKIE DOUGH:

| | |
|---|---|
| ¼ | cup plus 3 tablespoons unsalted butter |
| ¼ | cup plus 2 tablespoons confectioners' sugar, sifted |
| 1 | cup unbleached all-purpose flour |
| 1 | egg yolk |
| ½ | teaspoon vanilla extract |
| | Dash salt |

### MACADAMIA NUT TOFFEE FILLING:

| | |
|---|---|
| ½ | cup sugar |
| ¼ | cup (½ stick) butter, cut into pieces |
| ¼ | cup heavy (whipping) cream |
| ½ | cup macadamia nuts, coarsely chopped |

### GANACHE FILLING:

| | |
|---|---|
| 2 | ounces bittersweet chocolate, chopped |
| 1 | tablespoon heavy (whipping) cream |
| 1 | tablespoon Grand Marnier |

### MILK CHOCOLATE MOUSSE:

| | |
|---|---|
| 2 | ounces milk chocolate, chopped |
| ½ | cup heavy (whipping) cream |

### DARK CHOCOLATE MOUSSE:

| | |
|---|---|
| 4 | ounces bittersweet chocolate, chopped |
| 1 | cup heavy (whipping) cream |

### GLAZED BANANAS:

| | |
|---|---|
| ½ | cup sugar |
| 1 | drop fresh lemon juice |
| ½ | cup heavy (whipping) cream |
| 1 | tablespoon unsalted butter |
| 1 | banana, peeled and sliced |

### CARAMELIZED BANANA SABAYON:

| | |
|---|---|
| 6 | egg yolks |
| ½ | cup sugar |
| ¼ | cup crème de banana liqueur |
| ¼ | cup heavy (whipping) cream, whipped to soft peaks |
| | Glazed Bananas |

## DARK CHOCOLATE GLAZE:

| 2 | ounces bittersweet chocolate, chopped |
| 1/4 | cup simple syrup |
| 1/4 | cup nappage (apricot jam blended with pectin) |

## GARNISH:

| 2 | ounces bittersweet chocolate, chopped |
| 1 | cup fresh raspberries |
| 8 | Striped Chocolate Garnishes (page 184) |
| 8 | Pulled Sugar Leaves (page 185) |
| 8 | Pulled Sugar Spirals (page 185) |

*To make the pâte cigarette:* Preheat the oven to 375°F. Lay a sheet of parchment paper or buttered aluminum foil on a work surface. Lay a 24x14-inch piece of patterned metal mesh on top of the paper or foil as a stencil. In a large bowl cream the butter and sugar until fluffy. Gradually beat in the egg whites until well blended. Gradually beat in the flour and mix to a smooth batter. Blend in the vanilla. Pour half of the batter into a large bowl and stir in the cocoa until completely blended.

With a long, thin spatula, spread the chocolate batter across the stencil in a very thin layer. Use a squeegee to scrape across the back of the stencil, leaving the chocolate batter in the holes. Carefully lift the stencil. Lift the paper or foil and place on baking sheet pan. Put the pan in the freezer for 8 to 10 minutes, or until the design is set.

Put the pan on a work surface. Using a clean spatula, quickly spread the white batter in a 1/8 inch layer over the chocolate design, taking care not to disturb the chocolate layer. Bake for 7 minutes, or until very light brown. Set aside to cool slightly. Lay a sheet of parchment paper or waxed paper over the top of the cake and, grasping the top and bottom layers of paper, flip the cake over. Peel off the paper or foil to reveal the design. Let cool completely. Do not refreeze.

Line a baking sheet with parchment paper and place 2-inch tall by 4-inch diameter ring molds or PVC pipe sections on the paper. Cut flexible heavy plastic into 8 strips, each 3 1/3 inches wide and 12 1/2 inches long. Line each mold with a strip, which will stand 1 1/2 inches above the top of the molds. Make sure the ends meet.

Cut 8 strips of cake 12 inches long and 3 1/2 inches wide to fit the inside of the prepared ring molds. Gently roll the cake strip, pattern side out, and place it in the ring mold, unrolling it around the side of the mold. Make sure the ends meet but do not overlap.

*To make the sablés:* Line a baking sheet with parchment paper or lightly buttered aluminum foil. Preheat the oven to 350°F. In a large bowl cream the butter and sugar until light and fluffy. Gradually stir in the flour to blend. Add the egg yolk, stirring to blend completely. Stir in the vanilla and salt. Roll the dough out on a lightly floured board to a 1/8-inch thickness. Cut out eight 2 3/4-inch diameter disks. With a thin spatula, transfer the disks to the baking sheet and place in the oven. Bake for 8 to 9 minutes or until golden. Let cool. Remove the cookies from the pan with a spatula and press one into the bottom of each mold. They should fit snugly.

*To make the macadamia nut-toffee filling:* In a medium, heavy saucepan melt the sugar over medium-high heat, swirling until it turns a light golden brown. Remove from heat and swirl in the butter. Return to heat and stir in the cream. Add the nuts and stir to coat. Let cool. Place 1 tablespoon of filling in the bottom of each mold over the cookie.

*To make the ganache:* Put the chocolate in a medium bowl. In a heavy saucepan bring the cream to a boil. Pour the cream over the chocolate and stir together until melted. Stir in the Grand Marnier. Spoon 1 tablespoon in each mold over the filling.

*To make the milk chocolate mousse:* In a large double boiler melt the milk chocolate over barely simmering water. In a deep bowl whip the cream until it forms soft peaks. Stir a large spoonful of whipped cream into the warm chocolate, mixing thoroughly. Gently fold the remainder of the cream and chocolate together. Put the mousse in a pastry bag fitted with a medium tip and pipe a ¼-inch layer in each mold.

*To make the dark chocolate mousse:* In a large double boiler melt the dark chocolate over barely simmering water. In a deep bowl whip the cream until it forms soft peaks. Stir a large spoonful of whipped cream into the warm chocolate, mixing thoroughly. Gently fold the remaining cream into the chocolate. Fill the molds completely with the mousse and smooth the top with a thin spatula. The molds should now be filled to the tops of the plastic collars. Refrigerate for 30 minutes.

*To make the glazed bananas:* In a small, heavy saucepan melt the sugar in the lemon juice. Continue to cook the mixture until it is a light golden brown. Gradually pour in the cream, stirring constantly. Swirl in the butter and stir until melted. Remove from the heat and fold in the banana, stirring gently until coated.

*To make the sabayon:* In a double boiler over barely simmering water whisk the egg yolks and sugar together. Stir in the liqueur. Cook, stirring constantly, until the mixture thickens and coats the spoon. Let cool completely. Fold in the cream. Gently fold in the glazed banana slices.

*To make the glaze:* In a double boiler melt the chocolate over simmering water. Add the syrup and nappage and stir until smooth.

Remove the molds from the refrigerator. With a thin spatula, loosen the bottom of each mold from the paper. Lift the rings off the molds. Gently peel away the plastic collars. With a small spoon, spread 1½ teaspoons of glaze on the top of each torte, being careful not to let the glaze drip down the sides (if the glaze drips, skim it off with a kitchen knife or spatula). Return the tortes to the refrigerator to firm.

*To garnish and serve:* In a double boiler melt the chocolate over simmering water. Put the chocolate in a pastry bag fitted with a fine plain tip. Pipe 2 thin intersecting chocolate lines on the top border of the serving plate. With a spatula or your fingers, place a torte in the center of each plate. Pool 2 tablespoons of sabayon on one side of each torte. Pipe a dot of chocolate at the bottom edge of the torte and press one striped chocolate garnish into the chocolate, holding it for a few seconds until it holds firmly. Garnish with a few raspberries, a pulled sugar leaf, and a pulled sugar spiral.

# Chocolate and Raspberry Fontaine

*Jacques Torres*
LE CIRQUE
NEW YORK, NEW YORK

**SERVES 4**

| | | | | |
|---|---|---|---|---|
| 7 | ounces bittersweet chocolate, chopped | | 8 | sheets frozen filo dough, defrosted |
| ½ | cup heavy (whipping) cream | | 12 | disks (2½ inch diameter, ½ inch thick) plain |
| ⅓ | cup framboise liqueur | | | chocolate cake (white cake can be substi- |
| ½ | cup plus 3 tablespoons sugar | | | tuted) |
| ⅓ | cup boiling water | | 1 | pint raspberries |
| ½ | cup (1 stick) unsalted butter | | | |

☙ *Preparation:* Place the chocolate in a bowl. In a small saucepan heat the cream to boiling. Pour the cream over the chocolate and set aside until the chocolate melts. Stir to combine the cream and chocolate, then stir in 2 tablespoons of the framboise. Set aside to cool.

Dissolve ½ cup sugar in the boiling water; add the remaining framboise and set aside. In a small saucepan melt the butter. Spread one sheet of the filo on a work surface. Brush with some of the melted butter and place another sheet of filo over it. Brush with butter again and sprinkle with a teaspoon or so of sugar. Cut the double thickness of filo into 3 equal strips horizontally, each about 5 inches wide. Place a disk of chocolate cake in the center of each strip. Brush with some of the reserved framboise syrup and top with a generous spoonful of the chocolate and cream mixture. Place 8 to 10 raspberries of top, then fold the ends of the filo over the top, tucking them under. Fold the sides down and tuck them under, completely enclosing the chocolate and raspberry assembly. Repeat with the remaining ingredients, making 12 dumpling-like filo packages of raspberries and chocolate. There should still be raspberries left over. Place the packages on a baking sheet, brush them with melted butter, and sprinkle with remaining sugar. Refrigerate until shortly before serving time.

☙ *Presentation:* Preheat the oven to 350°F. Remove the pastries from the refrigerator and bake them about 15 minutes, until lightly browned. Cool about 5 minutes, then serve garnished with the remaining raspberries.

# Mocha Framboise

*Donna Nordin*
CAFE TERRA COTTA
TUCSON, ARIZONA

**SERVES 16**

CAKE:

| | |
|---|---|
| 14 | eggs, separated, at room temperature |
| 1¾ | cups sugar |
| 5 | ounces bittersweet chocolate, melted (semisweet or other high-quality dark chocolate can be substituted) |
| 1½ | cups walnuts, ground in a blender or food processor |
| 1 | teaspoon instant coffee dissolved in 1 teaspoon boiling water |

CHOCOLATE CREAM:

| | |
|---|---|
| 1½ | cups heavy (whipping) cream |
| 6 | ounces bittersweet chocolate, grated |

COFFEE BUTTERCREAM:

| | |
|---|---|
| 1 | cup sugar |
| ½ | cup water |
| 2 | eggs |
| 1½ | cups (3 sticks) unsalted butter, softened |
| 2 | tablespoons instant coffee dissolved in 2 teaspoons boiling water |

ASSEMBLY:

| | |
|---|---|
| ¼ | cup Framboise or other raspberry liqueur |
| ½ | cup strained raspberry jam |
| ⅓ | cup finely chopped walnuts |
| 32 | chocolate "coffee beans" |

☙ *To make the cake:* Preheat the oven to 375°F. Prepare two 10x15-inch jelly roll pans by greasing and flouring them, then lining the bottoms with parchment paper.

In the bowl of an electric mixer beat the egg yolks until light and fluffy. Slowly add 1½ cups of the sugar and continue to beat until the mixture is thick and forms a ribbon when it falls from the beaters. Divide the yolk mixture into two bowls; add the melted chocolate to one bowl and the ground walnuts and instant coffee to the second. Beat each well and set aside.

In a large bowl beat the egg whites at medium speed until foamy. Increase the speed to high and beat until stiff peaks form. Slowly add the remaining ¼ cup of sugar. Fold half of the meringue into each of the yolk mixtures and immediately pour the batters into the 2 pans. Bake for 20 to 30 minutes or until lightly browned.

Remove from the oven, cover the pans with tea towels, and let cool. Unmold and cut each lengthwise into two 5x15-inch pieces. Set aside.

☙ *To make the chocolate cream:* In a saucepan bring the cream to a boil. Remove from the heat, then stir in the chocolate. Place in the freezer until cool, then whip to a creamy consistency.

☙ *To make the coffee buttercream:* In a heavy saucepan cook the sugar and water until it reaches the soft ball stage, 240°F on a candy thermometer. In a large bowl beat the eggs, then slowly add the sugar syrup while beating, and continue to beat until the mixture cools. This can be done with a mixer or in a food processor. Beat in the soft butter bit by bit, then flavor with coffee extract. Chill until firm enough to handle, but do not allow it to become hard.

❧ *To assemble:* Start with 1 layer of chocolate cake and brush with the liqueur. Spread with all of the jam and a layer of coffee buttercream. Top with a layer of walnut cake and spread with half of the chocolate cream. Top with the second walnut layer and the remaining chocolate cream. Finish with the chocolate layer and end with the remaining coffee buttercream on the top and sides of the cake.

Mark the cake into 16 pieces and pipe a rosette on each side of each piece. Sprinkle the sides with chopped walnuts and place chocolate coffee beans on each rosette. Serve at room temperature.

❧ *Note:* The cake can be prepared up to 2 days in advance and should be stored in the refrigerator. Allow it to sit at room temperature for 2 hours before serving.

# Chocolate Roulade with Bittersweet Hazelnut Filling

*Rick O'Connell*

ROSALIE'S RESTAURANT
SAN FRANCISCO, CALIFORNIA

**SERVES 10 TO 12**

CAKE:

| | |
|---|---|
| ¾ | cup sifted unbleached all-purpose flour |
| ¼ | cup unsweetened cocoa |
| 1 | teaspoon baking powder |
| ¼ | teaspoon salt |
| 4 | eggs |
| 1 | cup sugar |
| ¼ | cup water |
| 1 | teaspoon vanilla extract |

FILLING:

| | |
|---|---|
| 1 | cup hazelnuts |
| 1 | cup ricotta cheese |
| ¾ | cup (1½ sticks) unsalted butter, softened |
| ¾ | cup sifted confectioners' sugar |

| | |
|---|---|
| ⅓ | cup half and half |
| 2 | teaspoons vanilla extract |

CHOCOLATE SAUCE:

| | |
|---|---|
| 1 | pound bittersweet chocolate |
| 6 | tablespoons unsalted butter |
| 1¼ | cups heavy (whipping) cream |
| ½ | cup milk |
| | Pinch salt |
| 1 | cup sifted cocoa |
| ¾ | cup light corn syrup |

GARNISH:

Confectioners' sugar
Fresh raspberries

☙ *To make the cake:* Preheat the oven to 350°F. In a medium bowl sift the flour, cocoa, baking powder, and salt together, and set aside. In the bowl of an electric mixer combine the eggs and sugar and beat about 10 minutes until the mixture is very thick and lemon-colored, and forms a ribbon when dropped from the beater. Add the water and vanilla to the egg mixture, then add the sifted dry ingredients in two stages.

Line a 10x15 inch sheet cake pan with parchment and spread the batter evenly over the paper. Tap on the counter to remove any air bubbles. Bake the cake for 12 to 15 minutes. Remove from the pan and trim to an even rectangle.

☙ *To make the filling:* Toast the hazelnuts in a 350°F oven for 10 minutes. Remove the nuts from the oven, place in a tea towel, and fold the towel over them so they are covered. Let them steam for 5 minutes, then rub the skins off while they are still inside the towel. Chop and set aside.

In the bowl of an electric mixer combine the ricotta, butter, and sugar, and beat until light and fluffy. Add the half and half and vanilla, then fold in the nuts.

Spread the filling over the cake and roll the cake tightly, using the lining paper as a guide. Refrigerate for a minimum of 1 hour with the seam side down on a platter.

∼ *To make the sauce:* Chop the chocolate coarsely. In a saucepan heat the butter, cream, and milk, and stir in the chocolate, syrup, cocoa, salt, and corn syrup. Heat, whisking constantly, until the mixture is combined and glossy. Set aside to cool and store in the refrigerator.

∼ *To serve:* Cut the roll into thin slices with a serrated knife and place 2 slices on each plate. Spoon the sauce around the slices and dust the top with confectioners' sugar and a few raspberries.

∼ *Note:* The cake can be made up to 2 days before serving, and the sauce keeps well in the refrigerator for 2 weeks.

# President's Cake

Dominique Leborgne
LE PALAIS DU CHOCOLAT
WASHINGTON, D.C.

**SERVES 8 TO 10**

## CHOCOLATE FLOURLESS CAKE:

| | |
|---|---|
| 1 | cup plus 6 tablespoons (2¾ sticks) butter, melted |
| 8 | ounces bittersweet chocolate, melted |
| 10 | egg whites |
| | Pinch salt |
| 2½ | tablespoons sugar |
| 6 | egg yolks |
| ⅓ | cup plus 1 teaspoon sugar |
| | Rum-flavored simple syrup (see Simple Syrup, page 186) |

## CHOCOLATE MOUSSE:

| | |
|---|---|
| 10 | ounces bittersweet chocolate |
| ½ | cup (1¼ sticks) plus 2 tablespoons butter |
| ⅓ | cup plus 1 teaspoon sugar |
| 2 | egg yolks |
| 6 | egg whites |
| | Pinch salt |
| ⅓ | cup sugar |

## TO DECORATE THE CAKE:

Melted dark chocolate
Melted milk chocolate

---

&#10148; *To make the chocolate flourless cake:* In a large bowl cream together the melted butter and melted chocolate. In a separate bowl beat the egg whites with a pinch of salt. When the egg whites reach the soft peak stage, add 2½ tablespoons of sugar and beat until stiff.

In another bowl beat the egg yolks with ⅓ cup plus 1 teaspoon sugar until the yolks are thick and the sugar is dissolved. Add the egg yolk mixture to the chocolate mixture. Fold in the egg whites. Pour the batter evenly into three 8-inch ring pans placed on a parchment-lined baking sheet. Bake at 350°F for 20 to 25 minutes. Allow the cake layers to cool. Soak the layers with rum-flavored simple syrup.

&#10148; *To make the chocolate mousse:* In the top of a double boiler over simmering water melt the chocolate. In a large bowl combine the butter and ⅓ cup plus 1 teaspoon of sugar. Add the chocolate and mix until incorporated. Add the egg yolks and mix well.

In a separate bowl beat the egg whites with a pinch of salt until soft peaks form. Add ⅓ cup of sugar and continue to beat until stiff peaks form. Fold the egg whites into the chocolate mixture.

&#10148; *To assemble the cake:* Place a cake layer in an 8-inch ring mold. Spread a layer of mousse over the cake. Brush with rum-flavored simple syrup. Repeat with the two remaining cake layers, ending with a mousse layer. Level the top layer of mousse with a spatula. Refrigerate until chilled. Remove the ring, and ice the outside edge of the cake with the mousse.

&#x4E; *To decorate the cake:* Cut a piece of plastic film (heavy, but flexible—not plastic wrapping film) to fit the outside edge of the cake. Using a comb, spread the plastic film with a thin layer of melted chocolate. When dark chocolate is set, top with a very thin layer of milk chocolate. Let set. Apply the strip around the cake, covering the entire outside of the cake.

Ladle melted dark chocolate onto a marble slab. Spread the chocolate very thinly with a spatula. When the chocolate has lost its sheen, scrape the chocolate into strips resembling ruffled ribbon.

Arrange the ruffled ribbons in one layer around the outer edge of the top of the cake. Repeat with a second layer just inside the first layer, overlapping slightly. Repeat the layers, working toward the center of the cake, until the entire surface of the cake is covered. Arrange some small pieces of ruffled chocolate in the center strip surrounding the cake. Refrigerate the cake until chilled and set. Sprinkle the top of the cake with confectioners' sugar.

# Flourless Macadamia Nut-Chocolate Cake

### Gerard Reversade

GERARD'S AT THE PLANTATION INN
LAHAINA, MAUI

**SERVES 8**

This dense cake can be baked a day ahead and finished on the day you plan to serve it. The chocolate, coffee, and macadamia nuts bring the Big Island to mind.

CAKE:

| | |
|---|---|
| 5 | *ounces bittersweet chocolate* |
| 1 | *cup macadamia nuts* |
| ¾ | *cup sugar* |
| 8 | *eggs, separated* |
| 1 | *cup unsalted butter, at room temperature* |
| | *Pinch salt* |

COATING AND GARNISH:

| | |
|---|---|
| 1½ | *cups heavy (whipping) cream* |
| 4 | *ounces bittersweet chocolate* |
| ⅔ | *cup (3 ounces) macadamia nuts, chopped and toasted (page 190)* |
| 1 | *tablespoon coffee extract* |
| 1 | *tablespoon Kahlua or other coffee-flavored liqueur* |
| 8 | *fresh strawberries* |

☙ *To make the cake:* Preheat the oven to 375°F. Place a round of parchment or waxed paper in the bottom of an 8-inch round cake pan or springform pan, and tie a collar of parchment or waxed paper around the sides to extend 2 inches over the top of the pan. Butter and flour the paper. Soften the chocolate by leaving it in a warm place for 10 minutes. Put the nuts and sugar in a blender or food processor and pulverize the nuts.

In the top of a double boiler beat the egg yolks until very pale in color. Place over barely simmering water to warm. In another pan over simmering water melt the chocolate. Stir in the butter until blended. With a wire whisk gently stir the chocolate into the yolks. With the same whisk, stir in the nut mixture until the sugar has melted.

In a large bowl beat the egg whites with the salt until they form stiff peaks. Stir ½ cup of the egg whites into the chocolate mixture to lighten it; then gently fold all the egg whites into the chocolate mixture. Transfer the batter to the prepared cake pan. Bake for 45 minutes or until a toothpick inserted in the center comes out clean. Let cool in the pan until just warm to the touch, then invert onto a wire rack and let cool completely to room temperature. The cake will deflate slightly as it cools. It can be covered and set aside overnight at this point.

☙ *To make the coating and garnish:* In a heavy, medium saucepan warm 1 cup of the cream over medium heat. Stir the chocolate into the cream until completely melted. Place the cake on a wire rack over a baking sheet, and pour the chocolate mixture over the cake, completely coating the top and sides. Smooth with a spatula. Let cool to firm slightly, then press the chopped macadamia nuts into the chocolate. Using a broad spatula, transfer the cake to a plate.

In a deep bowl beat the remaining ½ cup of cream until soft peaks begin to form. Beat in the coffee extract and Kahlua until stiff peaks form. Put the cream in a pastry bag fitted with a large star tip and pipe rosettes on and around the cake. Garnish with strawberries.

# Gâteau Nancy

Rene Verdon
LE TRIANON
SAN FRANCISCO, CALIFORNIA

**SERVES 24**

GÂTEAU:

| | |
|---|---|
| 14 | ounces semisweet chocolate, crumbled |
| 7 | ounces sweet butter |
| 2 | tablespoons Grand Marnier |
| 1 | teaspoon vanilla extract |
| 1 | tablespoon almond powder |
| 10 | egg yolks |
| 1½ | cups sugar |
| 10 | egg whites |

CRÈME ANGLAISE:

| | |
|---|---|
| 1½ | cups milk |
| 1 | 1-inch vanilla bean, split |
| 3 | egg yolks |
| ⅓ | cup sugar |

❧ *To make the gâteau:* In the top of a double boiler combine the chocolate, butter, Grand Marnier, vanilla extract, and almond powder, and heat over simmering water until melted. Remove from heat as soon as melted and whip lightly. In a separate bowl whip the egg yolks with ¾ cup of sugar for about 5 to 7 minutes until a white ribbon is formed. Blend into the chocolate mixture with a spatula. Whip the egg whites vigorously. Slowly add ¾ cup of sugar, whipping until lightly firm. Fold into the chocolate mixture, blending lightly as for a soufflé.

Preheat the oven to 275°F. Butter and flour two 10-inch round, 2-inch deep molds. Line with parchment, and butter the parchment. Pour half of the batter in each mold. Bake for 1 hour and 20 minutes. Unmold and cool on a rack.

❧ *To make the crème anglaise:* In a saucepan heat the milk with the vanilla bean to scalding. Allow to cool for 10 minutes. In a medium bowl beat the yolks with the sugar. Gradually add the hot milk, whisking constantly. Cook in a double boiler over simmering water, stirring constantly, until the mixture shows a "rose" pattern on the back of a wooden spoon. Cool over ice water.

❧ *To serve:* Sprinkle the gâteau with confectioners' sugar and serve with crème anglaise.

# Gâteau Chocolat Fondant

*Jacques Torres*
LE CIRQUE
NEW YORK, NEW YORK

**SERVES 8**

This flourless cake, meltingly soft on the inside, is served hot from the oven with freshly whipped cream, chocolate sauce, and a garnish of candied orange peel.

FLOURLESS CHOCOLATE CAKES:

½     cup (1 stick) unsalted butter, cut into pieces
     Pinch of salt
15    ounces bittersweet chocolate, preferably
      Valrhona, chopped
4     egg whites
½     cup sugar

GARNISH:

1½   cups heavy (whipping) cream
1      tablespoon confectioners' sugar, sifted
      Candied orange peel (optional)
2      cups Chocolate Sauce (page 188)

*To make the cake:* Preheat the oven to 400°F. Lightly butter and sugar eight 3-inch disposable aluminum tins, 2 inches deep. In a heavy, large saucepan melt the butter with the salt over low heat. Add the chocolate and stir over low heat until the chocolate is melted and the mixture is smooth. Be careful not to burn the chocolate. Let cool to room temperature.

In a large bowl beat the egg whites until foamy, then gradually beat in the sugar until stiff, glossy peaks form. Fold the egg whites into the cooled chocolate. Do not overmix or the batter will lose volume. Fill a pastry bag with batter and pipe into tins, filling each just over half full. Bake for 4 to 5 minutes. (It is important that the cakes are baked just before serving so the texture is correct. However, they can be made ahead and frozen before baking. Remove from the freezer at least 1 hour before baking.)

*To serve:* In a deep bowl whip the cream with the confectioners' sugar until stiff peaks form. Fill a pastry bag fitted with a star tip and pipe rosettes of the cream around the outer circle of the plates. Cut the orange peel into 1-inch strips and place 2 pieces crisscrossed between the rosettes, if you like. Turn the warm cakes out into the center of the plates and pour chocolate sauce over the top and around the sides.

# Chocolate Bourbon and Pecan Cake

John Draz
THE WINNETKA GRILL
CHICAGO, ILLINOIS

**SERVES 12**

CAKE:

12  ounces semisweet chocolate, chopped
1   cup (2 sticks) unsalted butter
8   eggs
1½  cups sugar
½   cup bourbon
1   pound pecans, finely ground just before use

GLAZE:

1   pound semisweet chocolate, chopped
⅓   cup vegetable oil

ASSEMBLY:

18  large pecan halves

*To make the cake:* Preheat the oven to 300°F. Butter the bottom and sides of a 12-inch springform pan. Place buttered parchment paper on the bottom of the pan and dust the bottom and sides with sugar. In the top of a double boiler melt the chocolate over simmering water. Cut the butter into small pieces and stir into the chocolate until melted. Set aside and keep warm. Separate the eggs. In a large bowl whip the egg whites until foamy. Add half the sugar and continue whipping until the egg whites are stiff. Set aside. Whip the remaining sugar and the egg yolks until ribbony. Mix in the melted chocolate and bourbon. Alternately fold in the ground pecans and egg whites. Pour the batter into the springform pan. Bake for 1 hour and 30 minutes to 1 hour and 45 minutes. Remove from the oven and cool.

*To make the glaze:* In the top of a double boiler melt the chocolate. Stir in the vegetable oil. Reserve.

*To assemble:* Remove the cake from the springform pan and invert onto an icing rack. Ladle glaze over the cake and spread to cover the top and sides. Garnish by placing pecan halves around the top rim. Refrigerate the cake for 30 minutes to allow the glaze to harden before serving.

# Chocolate Lover's Cake

*John Richard Twichell with Marcel Desauliniers*

TRELLIS
WILLIAMSBURG, VIRGINIA

**SERVES 10 TO 12**

Three chocolate textures in one dessert, with hazelnuts thrown in for good measure, make this a dream cake for chocolate aficionados. None of the three components of the recipe are difficult to make, and the cake may be assembled 1 day in advance and refrigerated, uncovered.

**CHOCOLATE CAKE:**

| | |
|---|---|
| 2 | tablespoons butter, melted |
| 1 | cup (2 sticks) unsalted butter |
| 8 | ounces semisweet chocolate, chopped |
| 10 | egg yolks |
| ½ | cup sugar |
| 6 | egg whites |

**CHOCOLATE MOUSSE:**

| | |
|---|---|
| 6 | ounces semisweet chocolate, chopped |

| | |
|---|---|
| 1½ | cups heavy (whipping) cream |
| 3 | egg whites |
| 2 | tablespoons sugar |

**CHOCOLATE GANACHE:**

| | |
|---|---|
| 1½ | cups heavy (whipping) cream |
| 20 | ounces semisweet chocolate, chopped |

| | |
|---|---|
| 2¼ | cups hazelnuts, peeled (page 190) |

*To make the cake:* Preheat the oven to 325°F. Lightly coat the insides of two 9-inch round cake pans with some of the melted butter. Line each pan with waxed or parchment paper, then lightly coat the paper with more melted butter and set aside.

In a double boiler melt 1 cup of butter and the semisweet chocolate over simmering water, stirring until smooth. Set aside at room temperature.

In the bowl of an electric mixer combine the egg yolks and sugar, and beat about 4 minutes until the mixture is slightly thickened and pale in color. Scrape down the sides of the bowl and beat for 2 minutes.

In a large bowl beat the egg whites until stiff peaks form. Using a rubber spatula, fold the melted chocolate mixture into the beaten egg yolk mixture. Add one-fourth of the beaten egg whites and stir to incorporate, then gently fold in the remaining egg whites.

Divide the batter among the prepared pans, spreading it evenly. Bake in the preheated oven for 45 to 55 minutes or until a toothpick inserted in the center comes out clean. Remove the cakes from the oven, and cool in the pans for 15 minutes. (During baking, the surface of the cakes will form a crust; this crust will collapse when the cakes are removed from the oven.) Invert the cakes onto the cake circles or flat plates. Remove the paper and refrigerate the cakes for 1 hour.

*To make the chocolate mousse:* In a double boiler melt the chocolate over barely simmering water, stirring until smooth. Remove from the heat, and set aside at room temperature.

In a deep bowl beat the heavy cream until stiff peaks form. Set aside. In a separate bowl beat the egg whites and sugar until stiff, glossy peaks form. Whisk one-fourth of the whipped cream into the melted chocolate. Fold the chocolate mixture into the egg whites gently but thoroughly. Cover and refrigerate.

*To make the ganache:* In a medium, heavy saucepan heat the heavy cream over medium-high heat. Bring the cream to a boil, stirring so that it does not boil over onto the stove. Place the chocolate in a stainless steel bowl. Pour the boiling cream over the chocolate, cover the bowl and let it stand for 5 minutes. Stir until smooth, and set aside at room temperature.

Chop the hazelnuts to $\frac{1}{4}$-inch pieces and chop in a food processor using an on-and-off pulsing action or chop by hand. Do not use a blender.

In a medium bowl combine $1\frac{1}{2}$ cups of the chocolate ganache and 1 cup of the chopped hazelnuts, and set aside at room temperature.

*To assemble and decorate the cake:* Spread the hazelnut-ganache mixture evenly over one cake layer, using a cake spatula. Place the other cake layer right side up on top of the ganache-covered cake. Press the cake layers together. Using a very sharp serrated knife, trim the top and sides of the cake so they are even. Refrigerate the cake for 30 minutes.

Remove the cake from the refrigerator and spread $\frac{3}{4}$ cup of the chocolate mousse evenly over the sides of the cake. Chill the cake in the freezer for 30 minutes or refrigerate for 1 hour.

Remove the cake from the freezer and pour the room temperature chocolate ganache over the cake, spreading it evenly with a spatula to cover the top and the mousse-coated sides of the cake. Refrigerate the cake for 20 to 25 minutes to set the ganache.

Transfer the remaining chocolate mousse to a pastry bag fitted with a No. 5 star tip. Remove the cake from the refrigerator and pipe mousse stars over the entire top of the cake. Press the remaining chopped hazelnuts into the ganache on the sides of the cake, coating the sides evenly. Refrigerate the cake for at least 1 hour before cutting and serving.

*To serve:* Cut the cake with a serrated slicer, heating the blade of the slicer under hot running water before making each slice. Allow the slices to come to room temperature for 10 to 30 minutes before serving.

# Cheesecakes, Pies, and Tarts

❧

## Chocolate Mousse Cheesecake

*Robert Krol*
CROZIER'S
METAIRIE, LOUISIANA

**SERVES 8**

Here's a chocolate cream cheesecake topped with a chocolate mousse. Are we chocoholics in heaven yet? For variations, try using chocolate cookies in place of vanilla wafers in the crust and sweet baking chocolate in the chocolate mousse.

CRUST:

| | |
|---|---|
| 15 | vanilla wafers |
| 2 | tablespoons sugar |
| 1 | tablespoon unsweetened confectioners' cocoa |
| 2 | tablespoons butter, softened |

FILLING:

| | |
|---|---|
| 6 | ounces semisweet chocolate, chopped |
| ¼ | cup (½ stick) butter |
| 20 | ounces cream cheese, at room temperature |

| | |
|---|---|
| 2 | eggs |
| 3 | egg yolks |
| 1 | cup sugar |
| 1 | teaspoon pure vanilla extract |

CHOCOLATE MOUSSE TOPPING:

| | |
|---|---|
| 6 | ounces semisweet chocolate, chopped |
| 1 | tablespoon rum |
| 2⅓ | cups heavy (whipping) cream |
| ½ | cup sugar |

✍ *To make the crust:* Preheat the oven to 350°F. Oil a 10-inch cheesecake pan. In a blender combine the vanilla wafers, sugar, cocoa, and butter, and grind until fine. Press the crust onto the bottom of the pan.

❧ *To make the filling:* In a double boiler over barely simmering water melt the chocolate and butter, stirring until smooth. In a blender or food processor combine the chocolate mixture, cream cheese, eggs, egg yolks, sugar, and vanilla until well blended. Pour over the crust. Bake for 35 minutes or until set. Let cool completely.

❧ *To make the topping:* In a double boiler over barely simmering water melt the chocolate with the rum and $\frac{1}{3}$ cup of the cream, stirring until smooth; set aside to cool. In a deep, medium bowl whip the remaining 2 cups of cream until stiff peaks form. Fold in the sugar and the chocolate mixture. Cover and chill. Pipe the mousse onto the cheesecake with a pastry bag. Chill for 2 hours.

# Kona Coffee–Chocolate Cheesecake with Macadamia Nut Crust

*Mark Hetzel*

THE FOUR SEASONS RESORT MAUI
WAILEA, MAUI

**SERVES 8**

A rich mocha flavoring from Hawaii-grown chocolate and coffee is blended with macadamia nuts and bananas in this dessert. The finished cheesecake resembles an individual torte, surrounded by a sea of caramel sauce. Other fruits and sauces can be used for variation.

## CRUST:

| | |
|---|---|
| 2 | cups unbleached all-purpose flour |
| ¼ | teaspoon salt |
| ¼ | teaspoon sugar |
| 7 | tablespoons cold unsalted butter, chopped |
| 3 | ounces bittersweet chocolate, grated |
| ¾ | cup lightly packed brown sugar |
| ½ | cup macadamia nuts, finely chopped |
| ½ | cup pecans, finely chopped |
| 6 | tablespoons freshly brewed double-strength Kona coffee |
| ¼ | teaspoon vanilla extract |

## CHEESECAKE FILLING:

| | |
|---|---|
| 6 | ounces bittersweet chocolate, chopped |
| 1 | cup heavy (whipping) cream |
| 3 | tablespoons ground Kona coffee |
| 1 | pound cream cheese at room temperature |
| ½ | cup plus 2 tablespoons sugar |
| 4 | eggs |
| ¼ | cup heavy (whipping) cream |
| 2 | tablespoons crème de cacao |

## SAUTÉED BANANAS:

| | |
|---|---|
| 3 | tablespoons unsalted butter |
| 2 | tablespoons packed dark brown sugar |
| 2 | ripe bananas, peeled |
| 2 | tablespoons Tia Maria liqueur |

## BANANA-CARAMEL SAUCE:

| | |
|---|---|
| 3 | bananas, peeled and diced |
| 3 | tablespoons orange juice |
| 1 | cup plus 2 tablespoons heavy (whipping) cream |
| 2 | cups sugar |
| ½ | cup water |
| 5 | tablespoons dark rum |

## CHOCOLATE GANACHE:

| | |
|---|---|
| 1 | cup plus 2 tablespoons heavy (whipping) cream |
| 4 | tablespoons unsalted butter |
| ⅜ | cup sugar |
| 3 | tablespoons unsweetened cocoa |
| 5 | tablespoons water |
| 9½ | ounces bittersweet chocolate, chopped |

## MACADAMIA NUT BRITTLE:

| | |
|---|---|
| 2 | cups plus 2 tablespoons sugar |
| 1 | cup Simple Syrup (page 186) |
| 1 | cup water |
| ¼ | teaspoon salt, dissolved in 2 tablespoons warm water |
| 2 | cups macadamia nuts |
| 1 | tablespoon unsalted butter |
| ¼ | teaspoon baking soda, dissolved in 2 tablespoons warm water |
| ¼ | teaspoon finely ground coffee |

&#10148; *To make the crust:* In a medium bowl blend the flour, salt, sugar, and butter with a pastry blender or your fingers until it is the texture of cornmeal. Add the chocolate, brown sugar, and nuts, and work with your fingertips until all ingredients are blended. Add the coffee and vanilla and mix to form a soft dough. Wrap in plastic wrap and refrigerate for 4 to 6 hours.

Preheat the oven to 350°F. Remove the dough from the refrigerator and roll out ¼ inch thick on a lightly floured surface. Using a 4-inch ring mold as a cutter, cut out 8 circles. Press the remaining dough into eight 4-inch fluted tart shells. Place the shells and circles on a baking sheet and bake in the oven for 8 minutes or until partially set. Let cool.

&#10148; *To make the filling:* In a double boiler over barely simmering water melt the chocolate and heat to 100°F. In a small saucepan bring the cream and coffee to a boil over medium heat. Strain through a fine-mesh sieve into the chocolate. Whisk until smooth and shiny.

Preheat the oven to 350°F. In a food processor or electric mixer beat the cream cheese and sugar together until light and fluffy. Beat in the eggs one at a time, scraping down the sides of the bowl with a rubber spatula and beating the mixture between each addition. Add the cream and liqueur and blend. Mix in the melted chocolate. Pour the mixture into the crust. Bake about 15 minutes until the center is just firm.

&#10148; *To prepare the bananas:* In a medium sauté pan or skillet melt the butter and brown sugar over medium-high heat. Cut the bananas into thin diagonal slices. Add the bananas to the caramel. Add the liqueur and sauté, tossing and stirring to coat all sides, until the bananas are just tender, about 1 minute. Remove from heat, pour out onto a plate, and let cool.

&#10148; *To make the sauce:* In a blender or food processor purée the bananas and orange juice. In a deep saucepan over medium-high heat bring the cream to a boil. Remove the cream from the heat and stir in the purée. In a medium sauté pan or skillet combine the sugar and water and cook over medium-high heat to a golden caramel color. Carefully pour in the hot cream mixture and cook for 3 to 4 minutes, stirring to blend. Strain the mixture through a fine-mesh sieve into a small bowl. Peel and cut the remaining banana into fine dice; you should have ¼ cup. Stir in the rum and diced bananas.

&#10148; *To make the ganache:* In a heavy, medium saucepan combine the cream, butter, and sugar, and bring to a boil. In a small bowl stir the cocoa and water to blend, then add to the cream mixture. Return the cream to a boil. Place the chocolate in a medium heatproof bowl and pour the boiling cream mixture over the chocolate to melt it. Gently stir the cream mixture and chocolate together. Keep warm over barely simmering water.

&#10148; *To make the brittle:* Oil a piece of marble or baking sheet. In a heavy, medium saucepan combine the sugar, simple syrup, and water and cook over medium heat to 236°F or until a small amount dropped into a glass of cold water forms a soft pliable ball. Stir the salt water into the mixture. Continue to 265°F, or until the same test yields a hard, pliable ball. Add the macadamia nuts and continue to cook to a light caramel color, 320°F. Remove from the heat, stir in the butter, baking soda mixture, and coffee, and pour out onto the prepared marble or baking sheet. Let cool. Break into large pieces and store in an airtight jar until ready to use.

*To assemble:* Line a baking sheet with parchment or waxed paper and place a wire rack on top. Place 4 sautéed banana slices on top of each cheesecake. Cover each with one of the baked cookies and press firmly into place. Unmold the cakes onto the wire rack, sealed side down. Pour ganache over the tarts to coat them completely. Let set, then carefully lift with a spatula and place on dessert plates. Surround each cake with sauce and stand a 5x3-inch piece of macadamia nut brittle in the top of each cake.

# Pumpkin-Chocolate Cheesecake

Alan Zeman
TUCSON COUNTRY CLUB
TUCSON, ARIZONA

**SERVES 12**

CRUST:

¾    cup graham cracker crumbs
3    tablespoons packed light brown sugar
5    tablespoons unsalted butter, melted
1½   teaspoons vanilla extract

SWIRL:

3    ounces bittersweet chocolate, chopped
¼    to ⅓ cup heavy (whipping) cream

FILLING:

2    8-ounce packages natural cream cheese, at
        room temperature
⅔    cup sugar
½    cup canned pumpkin (not pumpkin pie filling)

¼    teaspoon ground cinnamon
¼    teaspoon ground ginger
⅛    teaspoon ground cloves
¼    cup heavy (whipping) cream
5    eggs

MARZIPAN PUMPKINS:

(Makes 12)
4    tablespoons corn syrup
1    cup sifted confectioners' sugar
7    ounces almond paste
     Red and yellow food coloring
½    teaspoon water
12   whole cloves

❧ *To prepare the crust:* Preheat the oven to 275°F. In a medium bowl combine the graham cracker crumbs, brown sugar, butter, and vanilla, and press into the bottom of a buttered 9-inch square cake pan with 2-inch sides.

❧ *To prepare the swirl:* In the top of a double boiler, or in a bowl over simmering water, melt the chocolate with the cream. Stir until smooth and then set aside, keeping it warm.

❧ *To make the filling:* In the bowl of an electric mixer cream the cream cheese and sugar at medium speed, scraping the bowl frequently and beating until smooth. Add the pumpkin, spices, and cream, and then the eggs, one at a time, beating well after each addition. Pour the filling over the crust. Drizzle a spiral pattern with the chocolate over the top and draw it through the batter with a knife. Do not stir.

Place the cheesecake pan in a larger baking pan. Bake in the center of the preheated oven for 1 hour, or until the center is firm and not soupy. Cool at room temperature, then chill at least 2 hours.

ᵉ⬎ *To make the marzipan pumpkins:* Work the corn syrup, confectioners' sugar, and almond paste together to form a smooth dough, kneading it with your hands. Mix a few drops of red and yellow food coloring together with the water and add to the dough, kneading to evenly color it.

Form into 12 balls, then indent the top of each to form a pumpkin shape. Use the cloves to make pumpkin stems.

ᵉ⬎ *To serve:* Dip the bottom of the pan in very hot water for 1 minute. Invert onto a sheet of cardboard or a plate and then back onto a serving platter. Garnish each serving with a marzipan pumpkin, if desired.

# Bittersweet Chocolate Pie

*Kathleen Daelemans*
CAFE KULA
GRAND WAILEA RESORT, WAILEA, MAUI

**SERVES 6**

Guiltless, silky smooth, and rich tasting—this may be the perfect chocolate pie. This basic recipe can be garnished with different kinds of fruit and different colors of chocolate. Silken tofu is available in the Asian foods section of grocery stores; it is creamier than firm tofu. Fruitsource is a liquid sweetener.

CRUST:

| | |
|---|---|
| 10 | *low-fat graham crackers, broken* |
| 2 | *tablespoons maple syrup* |
| 2 | *tablespoons canola oil* |
| 2 | *tablespoons water* |

FILLING:

| | |
|---|---|
| ½ | *cup Fruitsource (available at natural food stores) or honey* |
| ¼ | *cup maple syrup or honey* |
| 21 | *ounces silken tofu* |

| | |
|---|---|
| 1 | *tablespoon vanilla extract* |
| ¾ | *cup unsweetened cocoa* |

GARNISH:

| | |
|---|---|
| ¾ | *cup Raspberry Purée (page 187)* |
| ½ | *cup banana slices* |
| 18 | *fresh raspberries* |
| 6 | *fresh mint leaves* |
| | *Unsweetened cocoa for dusting* |
| 6 | *tablespoons grated white chocolate* |

*To make the crust:* Preheat the oven to 350°F. In a food processor grind the crackers to fine crumbs. Pour into a medium bowl, add the remaining ingredients, and mix together until it forms a mass. Or, to make by hand, combine all the ingredients in a small bowl and stir together until the mixture forms a mass. Transfer the dough to an 8-inch pie pan and press with your finger to form a ¼-inch thick shell. Bake for 8 minutes or until set and lightly browned. Let cool in the pan.

*To make the filling:* In a medium saucepan over medium heat combine the Fruitsource and maple syrup or honey and cook for 5 minutes. In a blender or food processor combine this mixture and the tofu, vanilla, and cocoa, and blend until smooth. Pour the mixture into the cooled pie crust. Refrigerate for at least 2 hours or until firm but puddinglike.

*To serve:* Cut the pie and place slices on individual dessert plates. Sprinkle 2 tablespoons of raspberry purée on each plate and garnish with a few banana slices, 3 fresh raspberries, and a mint leaf. Sprinkle the rim of the plate with cocoa, and sprinkle 1 tablespoon of grated white chocolate over the pie.

# Rich Dense Chocolate Pecan Torte

*Elizabeth Terry*
ELIZABETH'S ON 37TH
SAVANNAH, GEORGIA

**SERVES 8**

### CARAMEL PECAN CRUST:

| | |
|---|---|
| 1 | cup (3½ ounces) pecan pieces |
| ⅓ | cup firmly packed light brown sugar |
| ¼ | teaspoon grated nutmeg |
| 2 | tablespoons all-purpose flour |
| 2 | tablespoons butter, chilled and cut into pieces |

### FILLING:

| | |
|---|---|
| 6 | ounces sweet chocolate |
| 2 | ounces bitter chocolate |
| 2 | egg yolks |
| 1 | scant cup heavy (whipping) cream |

### CHOCOLATE WHIPPED CREAM:

| | |
|---|---|
| 1¾ | cups heavy (whipping) cream |
| ¼ | cup sugar |
| 3 | tablespoons cocoa |
| 1 | teaspoon vanilla extract |

### BERRY PURÉE:

| | |
|---|---|
| 2 | cups strawberries and raspberries |
| 1 | to 1½ tablespoons sugar |
| 1 | teaspoon triple sec |
| 1 | tablespoon lemon juice |

### ENGLISH CREAM:

| | |
|---|---|
| 3 | egg yolks |
| 6 | tablespoons sugar |
| 1 | cup milk |
| 1 | tablespoon cornstarch |
| ½ | teaspoon vanilla extract |
| 2 | tablespoons heavy (whipping) cream |
| 1 | tablespoon triple sec |

Fresh strawberries
Fresh mint leaves

☞ *To make the pecan crust:* Preheat the oven to 325°F. Line an 8-inch springform pan with parchment paper. In the bowl of a food processor combine the nuts, brown sugar, nutmeg, flour, and butter. Process until the nuts are crushed and the butter is entirely incorporated. Spread the crumbs on top of the paper in the springform pan and press gently. Bake for 8 minutes. Remove the crust from the oven and let cool.

☞ *To make the filling:* In the top of a double boiler place the chocolates over hot water. Stir the chocolates until melted. Whisk in the egg yolks. Remove the pan from the heat. In a small saucepan heat the cream over medium heat until hot but not boiling. Immediately whisk the cream into the melted chocolate. When thoroughly combined, the mixture will be smooth with a rich dark brown color. Pour the filling into the prepared crust. Chill in the refrigerator at least 1 hour. Run a knife around the edge of the pan, and remove the sides. The torte should remain at room temperature for 15 minutes before serving.

&#9758; *To make the chocolate whipped cream:* Place the whipping cream in the well-chilled bowl of an electric mixer fitted with a well-chilled balloon whip. Whip on low speed until the cream is frothy. In a steady stream add the sugar and cocoa and whip, gradually increasing the mixer's speed until the cream begins to form peaks. Add the vanilla and whip until soft peaks form. Spoon the whipped cream into a pastry bag fitted with a metal tube.

&#9758; *To make the berry purée:* In the bowl of a food processor combine the strawberries and raspberries, sugar, triple sec, and lemon juice. Blend until liquid, and refrigerate until needed.

&#9758; *To make the English cream:* In a large heatproof bowl whisk together the egg yolks and sugar (the mixture will be very stiff). Add the milk and cornstarch, whisking until cornstarch is completely dissolved. Transfer the mixture to a large, heavy-bottomed saucepan, place over medium-low heat, and bring just to a boil. Simmer, whisking constantly, about 2 minutes until very thick. Transfer the hot pastry cream to a clean heatproof bowl and add the vanilla, cream, and triple sec. Cover the surface with buttered waxed paper. Chill the pastry cream at least 2 hours and up to 2 days. Whisk the pastry cream before using.

&#9758; *To assemble:* Pipe the whipped cream over the torte, completely covering the torte. Cut into individual slices and place on dessert plates. Spoon ⅓ cup of berry purée and ¼ cup of English cream onto each plate. Garnish with sliced fresh strawberries and fresh mint leaves.

# Chocolate Cream Pie with Meringue Crust

Kathy Ruiz
BISTRO GARDEN
HOUSTON, TEXAS

**SERVES 6**

CRUST:

| | |
|---|---|
| 3 | egg whites |
| | Pinch salt |
| | Pinch cream of tartar |
| ½ | cup sugar |
| ½ | cup chopped pecans |
| ½ | teaspoon vanilla extract |

FILLING:

| | |
|---|---|
| 9 | ounces bittersweet or semisweet chocolate |
| ⅓ | cup espresso |
| 4 | eggs, separated and at room temperature |
| 2 | cups heavy (whipping) cream |
| ¼ | cup confectioners' sugar |
| | Chocolate shavings for garnish |

*To make the crust:* Preheat the oven to 300°F. Lightly grease a 9-inch pie plate. In a mixer beat the egg whites with the salt and cream of tartar at medium speed until frothy. Increase the speed to high and slowly add the sugar, beating until stiff peaks form and the meringue looks glossy. Fold in the pecans and vanilla. Spread the mixture into the pie plate, building up a rim of meringue. Bake for 30 minutes, then cool at room temperature.

*To make the filling:* In a saucepan melt the chocolate. Remove the pan from the heat. Add the espresso, stirring until smooth, and allow the mixture to cool. Beat in the egg yolks, one at a time. Whip 1 cup of the cream until stiff and fold into the chocolate mixture. Beat the egg whites until stiff and fold into the chocolate mixture.

Pour into the baked pie shell and chill until set. Before serving, whip the remaining 1 cup of cream with the confectioners' sugar and spread on the pie. Sprinkle with chocolate shavings.

*Note:* If the pie is served the day it is baked the crust will remain crisp. It will become a chewy meringue by the next day.

# Chocolate Tart

### Maurice Delechelle
CROISSANT D'OR
NEW ORLEANS, LOUISIANA

**SERVES 6 TO 8**

Chocolate lovers will rejoice in this rich tart, which is gilded with caramelized confectioners' sugar and topped with a luxurious chocolate sauce.

TART SHELL:

1      cup (2 sticks) unsalted butter at room temperature
½      cup confectioners' sugar, sifted
1      egg
1      egg yolk
½      cup (2½ ounces) pecans, finely chopped
1      cup unbleached all-purpose flour

CHOCOLATE FILLING:

2      cups milk

1      tablespoon plus 1 teaspoon unsalted butter
8      ounces semisweet chocolate, chopped
1      egg

CHOCOLATE SAUCE:

1      cup heavy (whipping) cream
¼      cup hazelnut paste
2      ounces semisweet chocolate, chopped
6      tablespoons confectioners' sugar, sifted, for dusting

*To make the tart shell:* In the bowl of an electric mixer cream together the butter and confectioners' sugar. Add the egg and egg yolk, and beat until mixed. Add the pecans and flour, and beat to mix. Form the dough into 2 equal balls. Wrap and chill 1 ball of dough for 2 hours. Freeze the second ball of dough for later use.

Preheat the oven to 375°F. Roll the dough out on a well-floured board. Roll up the circle of dough onto the rolling pin and transfer it to a 9-inch tart pan with a removable bottom. Unroll the dough carefully, then roll the pin across the top of the pan to remove the excess dough. Press the dough into the pan around the edges. Bake for 15 minutes or until very lightly browned and crisp. Let cool. Leave the oven on.

*To make the chocolate filling:* In a medium saucepan combine the milk, butter, and chocolate and cook over medium heat, stirring constantly, just until the chocolate is melted. Let cool slightly, then whisk in the egg. Ladle the mixture into the cooled shell. Bake in the 375°F oven for 12 to 15 minutes, or until set.

*To make the chocolate sauce:* In a medium saucepan combine the cream, hazelnut paste, and chocolate. Place over medium heat, bring the mixture to a boil, and whisk until smooth and somewhat thick, about 10 minutes. Let cool, then transfer to a paper cone or a squeeze bottle for piping.

✎ *To serve:* Preheat the broiler. Dust the top of the tart with the confectioners' sugar and place 2 inches from the heat for about 10 seconds, or until the sugar is melted and lightly browned. Cut the tart into 6 or 8 pieces. Place 1 slice on each serving plate and pipe or drizzle the chocolate sauce over and around.

# Turtle Bay's Chocolate Banana Tart with White Chocolate Ice Cream

## Andrew Comey
TURTLE BAY RESTAURANT
COCKEYSVILLE, MARYLAND

**SERVES 8**

SWEET DOUGH:

½   cup (1 stick) butter
¾   cup confectioners' sugar
2   eggs
2   cups all-purpose flour
2   teaspoons vanilla extract

CHOCOLATE FILLING:

4   ounces unsweetened chocolate
½   cup corn syrup
1   cup sugar

4   eggs
½   cup (1 stick) butter, melted
3   bananas
4   ounces white chocolate

WHITE CHOCOLATE ICE CREAM:

5   egg yolks
1   cup sugar
3   cups light cream
14   ounces white chocolate
1½   cups heavy (whipping) cream

*To make the sweet dough:* In a large bowl cream the butter with the sugar. Add the eggs and mix well. Add the flour and vanilla, and blend until just combined. Refrigerate until firm.

*To make the filling:* In the top of a double boiler over simmering water melt the unsweetened chocolate. In a separate bowl mix together by hand the corn syrup, sugar, and eggs. Add the butter and chocolate, and stir until blended.

*To assemble the tarts:* Preheat the oven to 350°F. Roll the sweet dough to ⅛-inch thickness. Cut circles of dough to line eight 4-inch tart molds. Slice and roughly chop the bananas, and divide among the molds. Chop the white chocolate and sprinkle over the bananas. Pour the chocolate filling over the bananas and white chocolate, and fill to the top. Bake for 20 minutes or until set.

*To make the white chocolate ice cream:* In a large bowl mix the egg yolks and sugar until light in color. In a saucepan bring the light cream to a boil. Pour some of the cream into the yolk mixture. Return the yolk mixture to the pan and cook over low heat until thick enough to coat the back of a spoon. Place the white chocolate in a large bowl. Pour the light cream mixture over the white chocolate and stir until melted. Add the heavy cream and cool completely. Pour into an ice cream freezer and freeze according to the manufacturer's directions.

*Pumpkin-Chocolate Cheesecake*

*Kona Coffee-Chocolate Cheesecake with Macadamia Nut Crust*

*Meringue with Chocolate*

*Chocolate Brownie Soufflé*

*Double Chocolate Torte with Mascarpone and Wild Berry Chocolate Sauce*

*Lemon Cream Cappucino*

*Frozen Lime Ganache Parfait with Chocolate Tuiles*

*Chocolate Pâté*

# Dessert in All Simplicity

*Lucien Verge*
L'ESCARGOT
CHICAGO, ILLINOIS

**SERVES 4**

PASTRY:

1 cup all-purpose flour
2 tablespoons sugar
5 tablespoons unsalted butter, softened
2 egg yolks
  Dash salt

FRUIT GLAZE:

½ cup raspberries
½ cup sugar

CHESTNUT FILLING:

2 tablespoons chestnut purée
2 tablespoons chestnut spread

2 tablespoons unsalted butter, softened
2 tablespoons dark rum or kirsch
  Dash almond extract

CHOCOLATE GANACHE:

6 ounces semisweet chocolate
2 tablespoons unsalted butter
¾ cup heavy (whipping) cream

ASSEMBLY:

½ cup fresh raspberries (stemmed and halved
    fresh strawberries may be substituted)
  Confectioners' sugar

*To make the pastry:* On a pastry board or table make a well in the flour. Place the sugar and butter in the well and incorporate into the flour. Add the egg yolks and salt and work the dough until the ingredients are well blended and a smooth ball is formed. Cover the dough and let rest in the refrigerator for a few hours or overnight.

Preheat the oven to 350°F. On a floured board roll out the dough, adding as little flour as possible in the process, until it is the thickness of a silver dollar. Fill eight 4- to 5-inch oval tartlette molds with the pastry. Prick the bottoms of the pastry with a fork and fill each mold with any type of dried beans (to keep the shape of the mold while baking). Bake for approximately 15 minutes (remove the molds from the oven when the crust is slightly golden but is still soft in the center; the pastry will finish baking outside the oven). Let the shells cool slightly. Remove the dried beans. Unmold the pastry and reserve.

*To make the fruit glaze:* In a food processor or blender purée the berries with the sugar. Strain and reserve.

*To make the chestnut filling:* In a medium bowl mix the chestnut purée and chestnut spread with the butter. Add the rum and the almond extract. Reserve.

*To make the chocolate ganache:* In the top of a double boiler over simmering water melt the chocolate. Add the butter. Remove from the heat and whisk in the whipping cream. Reserve.

*To assemble:* Fill 4 of the pastry tartlettes with a mound of chestnut filling and place in the freezer for 15 to 20 minutes. Remove from the freezer and cover the tops with the chocolate ganache. Refrigerate for 15 minutes before serving. Brush the insides of the 4 remaining tartlettes with the fruit glaze. Arrange the fresh berries inside the pastry and dust with confectioners' sugar just before serving. Serve each person one fruit and one chestnut tartlette.

# Soufflés, Mousses, Terrines, and Other Divine Desserts

## Chocolate and Drambuie Soufflé

Vincent Vanhecke

INN AT PERRY CABIN
ST. MICHAEL'S, MARYLAND

**MAKES 8 INDIVIDUAL SOUFFLÉS**

FOR LINING SOUFFLÉ MOLDS:

2    *tablespoons unsalted butter*
1/3    *cup sugar*

SOUFFLÉ:

1    *cup milk*
1½    *ounces bitter chocolate*

4    *tablespoons unsalted butter*
   *Scant 2/3 cup all-purpose flour*
5    *egg yolks*
1/8    *cup Drambuie*
7    *egg whites*
2/3    *cup sugar*

Line the entire inside of 8 soufflé molds with the softened butter right to the top. Place the sugar in the molds and turn slowly so that the sugar sticks to all the butter. Reserve the molds in a cool place.

In a saucepan combine the milk and finely cut chocolate. Bring it to a boil over medium heat. While waiting for the milk and chocolate to boil, mix the butter and flour in a separate saucepan to make a beurre manie. Bring the beurre manie to a boil and whisk it to obtain a thick mix. Cook this mixture for 1 minute over medium heat, whisking constantly. Remove from the heat and add the egg yolks, whisking vigorously. Mix in the Drambuie.

Place the mix, now called panada, in a large mixing bowl and cover with plastic wrap.

In a separate mixing bowl whisk the egg whites until soft peaks form. Continue whisking and add the sugar gradually. Whisk until stiff peaks form.

Preheat the oven to 375°F. Fold one-third of the egg whites into the panada until a smooth mix is obtained. Add the remaining egg whites and fold in very gently until blended. Fill the soufflé molds with the mixture. Scrape the top flat with the back of a straight knife. Place the soufflés on an oven tray. Bake for 6 to 7 minutes. Remove from the oven, dust a little confectioners' sugar on top, and serve immediately.

*Chef's Tip:* Add a few drops of lemon juice to the egg whites before whisking. This will break down any fat that may be in the egg whites or mixing bowl.

# Frozen Soufflés Under a Chocolate Dome

## John Caluda

COFFEE COTTAGE
NEW ORLEANS, LOUISIANA

**SERVES 8**

In this spectacular presentation, scoops of frozen soufflés in three different sauces are hidden under chocolate domes that have been dusted with real gold. For a simpler dessert, forgo the domes and just garnish the soufflés with fresh berries.

### BASIC FROZEN SOUFFLÉ MIXTURE:

*(Makes 1 soufflé with one of the following flavors; repeat 3 times to make 3 soufflés.)*

| | |
|---|---|
| 2 | cups heavy (whipping) cream |
| 3 | eggs, separated |
| ¾ | cup sugar |

### FLAVORINGS:

| | |
|---|---|
| ¼ | cup green crème de menthe with 2 ounces white chocolate, melted |
| ¼ | cup Grand Marnier and Orange Zest Powder (page 191) |
| ¼ | cup grated dried coconut, ½ cup praline paste, and ¼ cup dark rum |

### CHOCOLATE DOMES:

| | |
|---|---|
| 2 | pounds good-quality semisweet coating chocolate, chopped |
| 8 | Mexican Balloons (see Note), optional Caramel, mango, and chocolate sauces (pages 187-188) |

☙ *To make the soufflés:* In a deep bowl whisk the cream until firm but not stiff peaks form. Place the egg yolks and sugar in the bowl of an electric mixer. Place the bowl over simmering water and whisk until the mixture is lukewarm. Beat the mixture at high speed until doubled in volume. Blend the crème de menthe and melted white chocolate into the whipped cream. Gently fold whipped cream into the egg yolk mixture. Pour into a 6-cup bowl and freeze. Repeat to make and freeze a second soufflé, flavoring it with Grand Marnier and orange zest powder. Repeat again to make and freeze a third soufflé, flavoring it with coconut, praline paste, and rum.

☙ *To make the domes:* In a double boiler over simmering water melt the 2 pounds chocolate and stir until cool to the touch but still liquid. Blow up the balloons until they are the proper size to make a dome that will cover the soufflés and sit on the serving plates to be used. Tie a knot in the top to hold the air.

Dip a balloon into the chocolate to a depth necessary to achieve the diameter needed. Tip it to evenly coat the sides if necessary. The coating should reach about 3 to 4 inches up the sides of the balloon. Lift the coated balloon from the chocolate and let the chocolate drain for a second, then turn it right side up and let the excess chocolate run down toward the base. Turn the balloon constantly to build up the thickness around the base of the dome. Your goal is to make chocolate shells thin enough to break with a spoon, but thick and firm enough to hold up while the dessert is being served. When the chocolate is thick enough, place the balloon knot end down in a container that will hold it without touching the dome. Chill or freeze for about 5 minutes, or until completely firm.

Remove the balloons when the chocolate is hardened and place them on a piece of waxed paper. Hold the knot between 2 fingers, pierce a balloon with a knife, and slowly release the air. The balloon may stick at the base, but it can be easily pulled loose. If a small hole develops in the dome, repair it with additional melted chocolate. If the dome crumples as the balloon deflates, the side wall may not have been coated thickly enough. Repeat to make the remaining domes.

In a separate small saucepan melt the milk and white chocolates over simmering water. Place each melted chocolate in a small pastry bag with a fine writing tip. Turn the domes over and drizzle lines of both chocolates over them. Lightly dust each dome with the gold dust. Place the domes in the freezer until ready to serve.

&#x25b6; *To serve:* Place about 2 tablespoons of each sauce on each dessert plate, spreading the pools out slightly. Place 1 scoop of the crème de menthe soufflé on each pool of chocolate sauce, 1 scoop of Grand Marnier soufflé on each pool of caramel sauce, and 1 scoop of coconut-rum soufflé on each pool of mango sauce. Garnish the center of each soufflé with a strawberry and place a dome over each plate.

&#x25b6; *Variations:* Substitute one or both of the following flavorings for one or two of the above flavorings: 2 tablespoons white crème de menthe mixed with 2 tablespoons crème de cacao, or ½ cup chocolate chips.

&#x25b6; *Note:* Mexican balloons seem to hold up best to the heat of the chocolate in this process, and are used by many chefs. Check party supply stores and departments, looking for balloon packages that say "made in Mexico." Gold dust for decorating food may be obtained from Albert Uster Imports, 1-800-231-8154.

# Chocolate Brownie Soufflé with Bitter Chocolate Sabayon

*Bradley Ogden*

ONE MARKET/LARK CREEK INN
SAN FRANCISCO, CALIFORNIA

**SERVES 6**

CHOCOLATE GANACHE:

2      cups heavy (whipping) cream
2      tablespoons sugar
2      tablespoons (¼ stick) unsalted butter
12    ounces bittersweet chocolate, chopped
6      ounces semisweet chocolate, chopped

BITTER CHOCOLATE SABAYON:

5      egg yolks
⅜      cup sugar
        Pinch salt
⅜      cup bourbon
¾      cup chocolate ganache (above)
1      cup heavy (whipping) cream

CHOCOLATE SOUFFLÉS:

10½   ounces bittersweet chocolate, chopped
1¼    cups cake flour
1      teaspoon baking soda
        Pinch salt
¾      cup (1½ sticks) unsalted butter
1      cup sugar
4      egg yolks
⅓      cup bourbon
1      tablespoon vanilla extract
¼      cup sugar
4      egg whites

        Confectioners' sugar for dusting

❧ *To make the ganache:* In a heavy, medium saucepan over medium heat combine the cream, sugar, and butter and warm until the butter is melted. In a large heatproof bowl combine the chocolates and pour the hot cream mixture over them. Let stand 5 minutes, or until all of the chocolate has melted. Stir gently to blend, Strain, cool, and cover. Set aside.

❧ *To make the sabayon:* In a medium bowl over gently simmering water combine the yolks, sugar, salt, and bourbon, and whisk about 4 minutes until thickened. The mixture will be custardlike. In a small saucepan melt the ganache over low heat. Transfer the egg mixture to the bowl of an electric mixer and beat on high speed. Add the ganache and whip until the mixture has cooled and the volume has increased. In a separate mixing bowl whip the cream until it stands in soft peaks. Gently fold into the chocolate mixture with a spatula. Cover and refrigerate.

❧ *To make the soufflés:* Preheat the oven to 350°F. Butter six 8-ounce soufflé cups. Sprinkle the inside with sugar, tilting the cups to coat all sides, then dump out the remaining sugar. In a double boiler over simmering water melt the chocolate. In a medium bowl sift together the flour, baking soda, and salt. Set aside. In another medium bowl cream the butter until fluffy. Beat in the sugar, one-quarter cup at a time. Blend in the egg yolks one at a time. In a small pan over low heat warm the bourbon. Stir the vanilla extract into the bourbon. Slowly pour the bourbon mixture into the egg mixture, beating until blended. Gently stir in the melted chocolate, stirring only until combined. With a spatula, fold in the flour mixture until blended. In a deep mixing bowl beat the egg whites with the remaining ¼ cup of sugar until soft peaks form. Very gently fold the egg whites into the chocolate mixture. Spoon the mixture into the prepared cups and level the tops with the back of a small knife. Bake for 20 to 30 minutes or until the outside is firm and the center is still soft.

*To serve:* Coarsely grind the chocolate espresso beans in a food mill or spice grinder. Remove the soufflés from the oven and let rest 5 minutes. Lift the top of each soufflé onto individual serving plates. Gently stir the sabayon to soften it slightly and place a large spoonful of sabayon onto each soufflé serving. Cover each with a top. Spoon more sabayon on one side of each soufflé. Dust with the ground espresso beans and confectioners' sugar.

# Chocolate Soufflé

*James Burns*
BISTRO
MT. PLEASANT, SOUTH CAROLINA

**SERVES 6**

### CHOCOLATE SOUFFLÉ:

| | |
|---|---|
| ¼ | cup all-purpose flour |
| ¼ | cup cocoa |
| 2 | cups heavy (whipping) cream |
| ½ | cup sugar |
| 1 | egg |
| 1 | egg yolk |
| 1 | tablespoon butter, at room temperature |
| 6 | egg whites |

### CHOCOLATE SAUCE:

| | |
|---|---|
| 2 | cups heavy (whipping) cream |
| 1 | cup (2 sticks) butter |
| 1 | cup firmly packed brown sugar |
| 1 | cup sugar |
| 1½ | cups cocoa |
| 1 | tablespoon bourbon |
| 1 | tablespoon vanilla extract |

### CHANTILLY CREAM:

| | |
|---|---|
| 1¾ | cups heavy (whipping) cream |
| ¼ | cup sugar |
| 1 | teaspoon vanilla extract |
| ½ | pint fresh raspberries for garnish |

*To make the chocolate soufflé:* Preheat the oven to 375°F. Butter 6 individual soufflé dishes and coat with a light dusting of sugar, tapping out the excess sugar.

In a bowl whisk together the flour and cocoa. In a heavy saucepan combine the cream and sugar and heat until it comes to a boil. Add the flour and cocoa, whisking briefly until smooth. Transfer the mixture to the bowl of an electric mixer fitted with a paddle attachment and beat until smooth. With the machine running add the whole egg, then the egg yolk. In a heavy saucepan heat the butter over low heat until melted. Cool. Add the butter to the mixing bowl, beating for an additional minute.

In the well-chilled bowl of an electric mixer fitted with a balloon whip, beat the egg whites with a pinch of sugar until the meringue just holds stiff peaks. Stir one-fourth of the meringue into the custard to lighten. Fold in the remaining meringue gently but thoroughly. Spoon the mixture into the prepared dishes. The soufflé may be prepared up to this point 1 hour ahead and chilled, covered with a paper towel and plastic wrap. Do not let the paper towel touch the surface of the soufflé. Place the cold soufflé in a preheated oven. Bake the soufflé dishes in the middle of the oven (make sure the rack is low enough to allow soufflé to rise about 2 inches) about 16 to 20 minutes or until firm and set in the center.

*To make the chocolate sauce:* In a small, heavy saucepan cook the cream, butter, and sugars over medium heat, stirring constantly, until sugar is dissolved and mixture is no longer grainy.

Remove the pan from the heat, add the cocoa, and stir until melted. Stir in the bourbon and vanilla, strain, and set aside to cool. If made in advance, the sauce may be reheated gently over low heat.

*To make the chantilly cream:* Place the whipping cream in the well-chilled bowl of an electric mixer fitted with a well-chilled balloon whip. Whip on low speed until the cream is frothy. In a steady stream add the sugar and whip, gradually increasing the mixer's speed until the cream begins to form peaks. Add the vanilla and whip until soft peaks form.

*To present:* Place individual soufflé cups on plates and accompany with chantilly cream, fresh raspberries, and a pitcher of warm chocolate sauce.

# Napoleon Pyramid

Daniel Bonnot

CHEZ DANIEL
NEW ORLEANS, LOUISIANA

**SERVES 4**

| | |
|---|---|
| 2 | 6x12-inch sheets puff pastry |
| | Sugar |

**CHOCOLATE MOUSSE:**

| | |
|---|---|
| 1 | pound Swiss chocolate, chopped |
| 2 | egg yolks |
| ½ | cup chocolate syrup |
| 4 | cups heavy (whipping) cream |
| 2 | cups sugar |

**GARNISH:**

| | |
|---|---|
| 1 | pint strawberries |
| 4 | tablespoons strawberry purée |
| 2 | ounces Chambord or other raspberry-flavored liqueur |
| 1 | cup brandied cherries |

☙ Preheat the oven to 375°F. Line two sheet pans with parchment paper or foil. Cover a flat work surface sugar. Lay out a sheet of puff pastry and coat the top with sugar. Using a rolling pin, press the sugar into the pastry. Turn over and repeat with the other side. Cut into 6 triangles. Place the triangles on the prepared pan and cover with another sheet pan to weigh them down. Repeat with the second sheet of pastry. Bake for 20 minutes. Remove from the oven, remove the top sheets, and let cool.

☙ *To make the mousse:* In the top of a double boiler over barely simmering water melt the chocolate. Remove the pan from the heat and stir in the egg yolks and chocolate syrup. Keep warm.

In a large bowl whisk the cream. After 1 minute, add the sugar and continue whisking until stiff. Add the chocolate mixture and blend until smooth. Put the mixture into a pastry bag fitted with a large star tip and refrigerate.

Trim the tops off the strawberries, cut them in half, and place in a small bowl. Add the strawberry purée and Chambord, then toss to coat the strawberries well.

☙ *To serve:* Pipe the chocolate mousse onto dessert plates in a triangular shape. Stand the puff pastry triangles up along the mousse to form a pyramid. Pipe mousse into the seams. Place strawberries on three sides of the pyramid and spoon cherries between the piles of strawberries.

# Chocolate Mousse with Harlequin Cookie Mask

*Kevin Graham*
WINDSOR COURT HOTEL
NEW ORLEANS, LOUISIANA

**SERVES 12**

Take yourself to Mardi Gras with chef Kevin Graham's Harlequin Cookie Mask. It makes a spectacular dessert presentation. You may, of course, prefer to serve his superb chocolate mousse out of costume—simply presented in an elegant glass container such as a cognac, Champagne, or parfait glass. Top with sweetened whipped cream and a few strategically placed raspberries.

CHOCOLATE MOUSSE:

| | |
|---|---|
| 1 | *pound semisweet chocolate, broken into pieces* |
| 4 | *large eggs, separated* |
| 1/3 | *cup water* |
| 1/3 | *cup dark rum* |
| 1/3 | *cup sugar* |
| 3 | *cups heavy (whipping) cream, whipped into peaks* |

HARLEQUIN MASKS:

| | |
|---|---|
| 1/2 | *cup all-purpose flour* |
| 1/2 | *cup confectioners' sugar* |
| | *Pinch cinnamon* |
| 1/2 | *teaspoon pure vanilla extract* |
| 4 | *egg whites* |
| | *heavy (whipping) cream, if needed* |
| 1 | *teaspoon unsweetened cocoa* |
| | *Vegetable oil spray* |

❧ *To make the chocolate mousse:* In the top half of a double boiler over simmering water slowly melt the chocolate. Place the egg yolks in a bowl then whisk in the water and dark rum. When thoroughly blended, stir in the melted chocolate.

In a large bowl beat 4 egg whites until foamy. Add the sugar and continue to beat until stiff peaks form. In a separate bowl beat the egg whites until stiff. Fold the beaten egg whites into the chocolate mixture, then fold in the whipped cream. Spoon into serving glasses and chill.

❧ *To make the harlequin masks:* Trace a mask shape about 7 inches long onto a piece of cardboard, making sure that you allow a border. Cut the shape out, leaving a mask stencil with straight edges and a 2-inch border all around. Cut around the eyes, leaving them attached to the upper edge of the stencil by a thin strip of cardboard.

In a large bowl sift the flour and confectioners' sugar together. With an electric mixer on low speed, add the cinnamon and vanilla, then the egg whites, one by one, mixing well to make a paste. Let the mixture sit in the bowl for 45 minutes at room temperature. (If the paste is still thick after 45 minutes, thin with a small amount of heavy cream.) Mix 2 tablespoons of the paste with the cocoa and place in a pastry bag with a narrow tip. Set aside.

Preheat the oven to 375°F. Cover a baking sheet with parchment paper and spray lightly with vegetable oil spray. Lay the mask stencil on top of the greased paper. Using a spatula, spread a thin layer of paste over the mask. Lift the stencil and repeat to make twelve masks in all. Using the pastry bag, pipe a thin band of chocolate paste $\frac{1}{2}$ inch wide along the edge of each mask. Draw a toothpick through the chocolate band using an up-and-down motion to create a decorative effect resembling feathers. Place in the preheated oven and bake for 10 minutes or until the dough begins to turn golden. Remove from the oven and immediately peel each mask, one at a time, off the paper. Place a large canister on its side and wrap the masks around the canister to give them a curved shape. Let cool on the canister before handling. The masks can be stored in an airtight container for up to 8 hours.

*To serve:* Prop each mask against a tall champagne or martini glass filled with chocolate mousse.

# Caramelized Pears with Chocolate Mousse in a Tulipe

Philippe Kaemmerlé

FRENCH CULINARY INSTITUTE/L'ÉCOLE
NEW YORK, NEW YORK

### SERVES 4

This dessert has all of the flavors of spring and would make a wonderful ending to an Easter dinner. The pears are carved into the shape of eggs, poached, and coated with caramel sauce. They surround a very light chocolate mousse in a crisp cookie cup.

## POACHED PEARS:

| | |
|---|---|
| 4 | large pears |
| 3 | cups water |
| 1 | cup dry white wine |
| 1 | cup sugar |
| 1 | tablespoon grated orange zest |
| 2 | cloves |
| ¼ | teaspoon ground nutmeg |
| 1 | cinnamon stick, broken in half |

## CHOCOLATE MOUSSE:

| | |
|---|---|
| 2½ | ounces semisweet chocolate, chopped |
| ¾ | cup heavy (whipping) cream |
| 2 | egg whites |
| 1 | tablespoon sugar |

## TULIPE COOKIES:

| | |
|---|---|
| 5 | tablespoons unsalted butter, at room temperature |
| 5 | tablespoons confectioners' sugar, sifted |
| 2 | egg whites |
| 3 | tablespoons cake flour |

## CHOCOLATE BUTTERFLIES (OPTIONAL):

| | |
|---|---|
| 2 | ounces semisweet chocolate, chopped |

## GARNISH:

| | |
|---|---|
| 1 | cup Caramel Sauce (page 188) |
| 2 | tablespoons cognac |
| 20 | fresh strawberries, hulled and halved |
| ½ | cup pistachio nuts, finely chopped |
| 4 | fresh mint sprigs |

◆ *To prepare the pears:* Cut each into 5 even sections and carve each piece into an egg-shaped oval with a paring knife. In a medium saucepan combine the water, wine, sugar, orange zest, cloves, nutmeg, and cinnamon stick, and bring to a boil over medium heat. Simmer the liquid for 5 minutes, then add the pears and cook for 20 to 25 minutes or until the pears are tender.

◆ *To make the mousse:* In a large bowl set over a pan of barely simmering water melt the chocolate, stirring until smooth. Set aside. In a deep bowl beat the heavy cream until it holds soft peaks and set aside. In a large bowl beat the egg whites until foamy, then add the sugar and beat until stiff, glossy peaks are formed. Fold the beaten whites into the melted chocolate, then fold in the whipped cream. Cover and chill until needed.

❧ *To make the cookies:* In a medium bowl beat the butter and the confectioners' sugar until light and fluffy. Slowly add the egg whites and the cake flour, mixing until fully incorporated.

Preheat the oven to 350°F. Lightly grease a baking sheet with butter, then dust it with flour. Drop 1 tablespoonful of dough onto the baking sheet and spread it with a thin metal spatula into a circle 4 inches in diameter. Repeat, distributing the cookies evenly across the baking sheet, leaving 3 inches between them. Bake the cookies about 5 to 8 minutes until they are golden brown. Working quickly, mold the warm cookies over a small glass or custard cup to form 2-inch-diameter cups. Return the baking sheet to the oven to warm the cookies if they are too stiff to mold. Let the cookie bowls cool, then invert and set aside.

❧ *To make the chocolate butterflies:* Draw an outline of a butterfly on a piece of waxed paper or parchment paper. Fold another small piece of paper in half, then lay it over the drawing, smoothing out the fold and making sure that the folded line is in the center of the butterfly drawing. Melt the chocolate in a double boiler over barely simmering water, stirring until smooth. Let cool slightly, then transfer the chocolate to a parchment paper cone, then snip the end. Trace the outline of the butterfly drawing, then transfer the chocolate outline to the refrigerator until needed. Repeat to make 3 more butterflies. (Kaemmerlé places his chocolate butterfly in special V-shaped molds to shape them.) Transfer the chilled chocolate mousse to a pastry bag with a fluted star tip. Fill the cookie bowls with the chocolate mousse and chill until firm.

❧ *To assemble the dessert:* In a saucepan warm the caramel sauce and add the cognac, stirring to incorporate. Add the pears, stirring gently to coat them evenly. Place a cookie bowl in the center of each plate. Arrange 5 pear pieces in a star pattern around each cookie bowl and drizzle some caramel sauce over the pears. Place 10 strawberry halves between the pear pieces, then sprinkle the pears with the chopped pistachios. Perch a chocolate butterfly on the edge of each chocolate mousse. Garnish with the mint sprigs, and serve.

❧ *Note:* All the components of this dish may be prepared 1 day in advance. Keep the cookie bowls in an airtight container, and cover and refrigerate the pears, mousse, caramel sauce, and chocolate butterflies.

# Double-Chocolate Torte with Mascarpone Mousse and Wild Berry-Chocolate Sauce

*Todd Rogers*
THE DINING ROOM
THE RITZ-CARLTON, HOUSTON, TEXAS

**SERVES 12 TO 16**

This could be the ultimate Texas dessert: a slice of chocolate torte with a heart of white chocolate terrine and a coating of chocolate ganache, topped a with a chocolate oil rig filled with Mascarpone mousse and spouting a "Texas tea" of berry and chocolate sauce.

CHOCOLATE TORTE:

| | |
|---|---|
| 20 | egg yolks |
| 3¼ | cups sugar |
| 2¼ | cups (4½ sticks) unsalted butter |
| 18 | ounces semisweet chocolate, chopped |
| 12 | egg whites |

WHITE CHOCOLATE MOUSSE:

| | |
|---|---|
| 8 | ounces white chocolate, chopped |
| ½ | cup sugar |
| 6 | tablespoons water |
| 3 | envelopes plain gelatin |
| 3 | cups heavy (whipping) cream |
| ¼ | cup pistachio nuts, chopped |

MASCARPONE MOUSSE:

| | |
|---|---|
| 1 | pound Mascarpone cheese at room temperature |
| ¾ | cup sugar |
| 4 | cups heavy (whipping) cream |

CHOCOLATE OIL RIGS AND SPROUTS:

| | |
|---|---|
| 2 | pounds semisweet chocolate, chopped |

WILD BERRY–CHOCOLATE SAUCE:

| | |
|---|---|
| 4 | cups water |
| 3½ | cups sugar |
| 5 | tablespoons cornstarch |
| ½ | cup dark rum |
| 1½ | cups unsweetened cocoa |
| 6 | ounces semisweet chocolate, finely chopped |
| 1 | cup each fresh raspberries, blueberries, and blackberries |

GANACHE:

| | |
|---|---|
| 12 | ounces semisweet chocolate, chopped |
| 1 | cup heavy (whipping) cream |

GARNISH:

| | |
|---|---|
| 2 | cups each fresh raspberries, blueberries, and blackberries |
| 12 | to 16 fresh mint sprigs |

❧ *To make the chocolate torte:* Preheat the oven to 350°F. Line a 13x17-inch sided baking pan with parchment paper or waxed paper. In a large bowl beat the egg yolks until they are pale yellow and a slowly dissolving ribbon is formed on the surface of the yolks when the beater or whisk is lifted. Blend in the sugar. In a double boiler over simmering water melt the butter and chocolate. Stir until smooth, then blend the chocolate mixture into the egg mixture.

In a large bowl beat the egg whites until stiff, glossy peaks form, then fold them into the chocolate mixture. Spread the batter onto the prepared pan and bake for about 30 minutes, or until a toothpick inserted in the center comes out clean. Let cool for 10 minutes, then invert and unmold onto a sheet of parchment paper or waxed paper. Scrape the top of the cake to remove the crust. Set aside.

⌘ *To make the white chocolate mousse:* Line a 6-cup semicircular terrine, no deeper than 2 inches, with plastic wrap. In a double boiler over simmering water melt the chocolate and sugar, stirring to dissolve for about 3 minutes. Add the gelatin mixture to the chocolate and stir until smooth. Let cool slightly.

In a deep bowl whip the cream until stiff peaks form, then fold in the pistachio nuts. Fold the chocolate mixture into the whipped cream. Pour the mousse into the prepared terrine. Cover and freeze at least 4 to 5 hours or overnight.

⌘ *To make the Mascarpone mousse:* In a large bowl whisk the cheese and sugar together until the sugar is dissolved. In a deep bowl whip the heavy cream until stiff peaks form, then fold into the Mascarpone mixture. Place in a pastry bag with a plain tip and refrigerate until needed.

⌘ *To make the oil rigs and spouts:* In a double boiler over simmering water, melt the chocolate until smooth. Draw 4 equal sides of an oil rig on paper. Cover each with an acetone plastic sheet and pipe the chocolate outline of the oil rig. Let cool to harden. The oil spout can also be drawn freehand in a fountain or featherlike shape and piped as above on an acetone sheet. Make 12 to 16 rigs (4 sides each) and sprouts.

To assemble the oil rigs, place 2 sides at right angles with long edges together, and "glue" them with additional melted chocolate piped on the inside edges. Hold in place to let the chocolate cool and firm. Repeat with the remaining 2 sides, then "glue" the 4 sides together into a tower. Repeat with the remaining sides to form all rigs.

⌘ *To make the wild berry–chocolate sauce:* In a medium saucepan combine 3 cups of the water and the sugar and bring to a boil over medium heat. In a small bowl dissolve the cornstarch in the remaining water and add the rum. Whisk the cornstarch mixture into the boiling sugar syrup. Add the cocoa and stir until the mixture is thickened.

Meanwhile, in a double boiler over simmering water melt the chocolate. Remove the rum mixture from the heat and stir in the melted chocolate. Strain the berries through a fine-mesh sieve, pushing them through with the back of a large spoon. Add the berry purée to the chocolate mixture. Let cool, then strain the sauce through a fine-mesh sieve.

⌘ *To make the ganache:* In a double boiler over simmering water melt the chocolate with the cream, whisking gently to a smooth consistency. Let cool slightly to a pourable consistency.

⌘ *To assemble the cake roll:* Remove the white chocolate terrine from the freezer and unmold onto parchment paper or waxed paper. Remove the plastic wrap and cut the cake to the proper length to encircle the terrine. Place the terrine at one edge of the cake and, with the aid of the parchment or waxed paper, roll the cake around the terrine to encase it, placing the seam on the flat side of the terrine. Trim the ends of the cake flush with the terrine. Place the cake roll flat side down. Coat the top and sides of the cake roll with ganache and return it to the freezer to firm up.

*To serve:* Remove the cake roll from the freezer and cut it into $3/4$-inch thick slices. Place one slice on each dessert plate and stand an oil rig alongside. Fill the rigs with the Mascarpone mousse, piping it in from the top. Place the fresh berries around the edge of the plates. Ladle the sauce down the sides of the rigs and around the plate over the berries. Garnish with fresh mint and stand a chocolate spout in the mousse at the top of each rig.

# Chocolate-Toffee Mountains

George Bozko
AMERICAN SEASONS
NANTUCKET, MASSACHUSETTS

**SERVES 8**

Although these are not high mountains, they are certainly rich ones, with two chocolate sauces and a caramel sauce napping the individual chocolate-robed tortes. The tortes are similar to baked mousses, and are moist and delicious on their own, even without the sauces.

CHOCOLATE TORTES:

8    ounces bittersweet chocolate, chopped
1    cup (2 sticks) unsalted butter
1½   cups firmly packed dark brown sugar
¾    cup unsweetened cocoa
6    eggs
½    cup freshly brewed coffee
1    cup slivered almonds, toasted (page 190)

CHOCOLATE GLAZE:

10   ounces semisweet chocolate, chopped
1¼   cups heavy (whipping) cream
3    tablespoons corn syrup
2    teaspoons cognac
1½   teaspoons vanilla extract

WHITE CHOCOLATE SAUCE:

1½   pounds white chocolate, chopped
1½   cups heavy (whipping) cream

2    tablespoons Triple Sec or other orange-
     flavored liqueur

DARK CHOCOLATE SAUCE:

1    cup water
1    cup sugar
¼    cup corn syrup
3    tablespoons unsweetened cocoa
4    ounces semisweet chocolate, chopped
1½   cups heavy (whipping) cream

GARNISH:

8    ounces Almond Roca candy
4    ounces semisweet chocolate, chilled
     Caramel Sauce (page 188)

🍃 *To make the chocolate tortes:* Preheat the oven to 300°F. Grease eight 4-ounce fluted molds with butter. In a double boiler over barely simmering water melt the chocolate and butter, stirring until smooth. Set aside. In a medium bowl combine the brown sugar and cocoa. Add the eggs, coffee, and almonds, and beat until well blended. Add the melted chocolate mixture and blend in. Divide the batter among the prepared molds. Place the filled molds in a baking pan, then fill the baking pan with enough hot water to come halfway up the side of the molds. Bake in the preheated oven for 40 to 50 minutes until just set. The edges will be dry, but the center will not be fully cooked; do not overbake or the tortes will be dry. Allow the tortes to cool for 10 minutes. Turn out onto wire racks, let cool slightly, then refrigerate for 1 hour.

*To make the chocolate glaze:* Place the chocolate in a medium bowl. In a small saucepan combine the cream, corn syrup, cognac, and vanilla, and bring to a boil. Pour the hot liquid over the chocolate and let the mixture stand for 2 minutes. Stir until melted and smooth, then strain through a fine-mesh sieve and set aside.

*To make the white chocolate sauce:* Place the chocolate in a large bowl. In a medium saucepan bring the heavy cream to a boil. Stir in the Triple Sec or other liqueur and pour this mixture over the white chocolate. Stir until melted and smooth. Strain through a fine-mesh sieve and set aside.

*To make the dark chocolate sauce:* In a medium saucepan combine the water, sugar, and corn syrup over medium heat. Bring to a boil and cook for 1 minute. Stir in the cocoa, return to a boil, and cook for 1 additional minute. Repeat with the chopped chocolate and cream. Strain through a fine-mesh sieve and set aside.

Spoon the chocolate glaze over the chilled tortes and refrigerate them for 15 minutes. Place the Almond Roca candy in a heavy plastic bag and hit it with a smooth side of a meat mallet or bottom of a heavy pot until ¼-inch shards are formed. Shave the chocolate with a vegetable peeler to make ¼ cup of shavings. To serve, pool caramel sauce in the middle of each plate. Place 1 torte in the center of each pool of caramel, then pour white chocolate sauce down one side of the torte and dark chocolate down the other side. Garnish with the candy shards and chocolate shavings.

*Note:* The tortes and sauces may be made up to a day in advance, then covered and refrigerated separately. Heat the sauces over low heat until liquid and smooth before serving. The chef uses a large quantity of sauce for each dessert; the amounts may easily be cut in half.

# Meringue with Chocolate

*Francesco Ricchi*

I RICCHI
WASHINGTON, D.C.

**SERVES 4 TO 6**

**MERINGUE SHELLS:**

| | |
|---|---|
| 3 | cups confectioners' sugar |
| 1½ | cups cocoa |
| 7 | egg whites |
| 1⅓ | cups sugar |

**MERINGUE FILLING:**

| | |
|---|---|
| 2 | quarts whipped cream |
| 1 | scant cup sugar |
| 1½ | scant cups cocoa |

✑ *To make the meringue shells:* In a medium bowl mix the confectioners' sugar and cocoa. In a large bowl whip the egg whites and sugar for 7 to 8 minutes until firm peaks form. Using a spatula, incorporate the confectioners' sugar and cocoa mixture into the egg whites and sugar. Mix well.

Mark pan liners with 8-inch circles using pencil. Place the meringue mixture in a pastry bag. Starting from the center point of a circle, swirl the meringue mixture around the circle in a spiral until the circle is filled. Bake at 300°F for 2 hours.

✑ *To make the meringue filling:* In a large bowl using a whisk, mix the whipped cream, sugar, and cocoa together. Then use an electric mixer for 2 to 3 minutes until it is fluffy (be careful not to overmix).

✑ *To assemble:* Using the 8-inch cardboard cake form, trim the meringue disk to fit the form. Using a pastry bag, layer the disk with a layer of filling. Place the second disk on top and repeat with a layer of filling. Using a spatula, cover the sides with the meringue filling. With the crumbs left from the trimmed disks, coat the side and the top. Wrap in plastic and place in the freezer.

The meringue needs 3 hours to set, but can be stored longer. Remove 1 hour prior to serving.

# Chocolate–Macadamia Nut Meringue with Tropical Fruit Cream

*Thomas Worhach*

THE OCEAN GRAND
PALM BEACH, FLORIDA

**SERVES 12**

This elaborate Caribbean dessert fantasy layers a chewy chocolate meringue with mango and guava creams, toffee crunch, ganache, and chocolate glaze. The garnish gilds the lily by adding a variety of sauces, sorbets, and fresh fruit.

### CHOCOLATE–MACADAMIA NUT MERINGUE:

| | |
|---|---|
| 2 | cups egg whites (about 8 to 10) |
| 2 | cups sugar |
| 1 | pound macadamia nuts, toasted (page 000) |
| 1 | pound semisweet chocolate, chopped |

### MANGO CREAM:

| | |
|---|---|
| 2 | mangos |
| 3 | tablespoons sugar |
| 2 | cups heavy (whipping) cream |
| 1½ | tablespoons (1½ envelopes) plain gelatin |
| 2 | tablespoons water |

### GUAVA CREAM:

| | |
|---|---|
| 3 | guavas |
| 3 | tablespoons sugar |
| 2 | cups heavy (whipping) cream |
| 1½ | tablespoons plain gelatin |
| 2 | tablespoons water |

### CHOCOLATE GANACHE:

| | |
|---|---|
| 2 | pounds semisweet chocolate, chopped |
| 4 | cups heavy (whipping) cream |
| ¼ | cup sugar |

### CHOCOLATE GLAZE:

| | |
|---|---|
| 1½ | pounds semisweet chocolate, chopped |
| 1 | pound (4 sticks) unsalted butter |
| ½ | cup dark rum |
| ¼ | cup light corn syrup |

### TOFFEE CRUNCH:

| | |
|---|---|
| 2 | Heath candy bars |

### CHOCOLATE FINISH:

| | |
|---|---|
| 6 | ounces white chocolate, chopped |
| 6 | ounces milk chocolate, chopped |

### GARNISH:

| | |
|---|---|
| | Mango, blackberry, guava, and raspberry sauces (page 187) |
| 1 | cup Crème Fraîche (page 187) |
| 1 | quart passion fruit sorbet |
| 1 | quart raspberry sorbet |
| 24 | fresh raspberries |
| 12 | fresh strawberries, hulled |
| 12 | fresh plum wedges |

❧ *To make the meringue:* Heat the oven to 325°F. Lightly spray a 13x17-inch sided baking sheet with vegetable oil spray and line it with parchment paper or waxed paper. In a large bowl beat the egg whites until foamy, then gradually beat in 1 cup of the sugar until stiff peaks form.

In a blender or food processor grind the nuts with the remaining 1 cup sugar. Fold the two mixtures together and spread evenly in the prepared pan.

Bake for 25 to 30 minutes, or until golden brown. Let cool and remove from pan. In a double boiler over simmering water, melt the chocolate and spread evenly over the top of the meringue. Let the chocolate set, then cut the meringue into 3 lengthwise strips. Set aside.

*To make the mango cream:* Peel, pit, and coarsely chop 1 of the mangos and purée in a blender or food processor until smooth. Strain through a fine-mesh sieve and add 1 tablespoon of the sugar. In a deep bowl whip the cream until stiff peaks form. Fold in the mango purée.

Peel, pit, and cut the remaining mango into ¼-inch dice. Toss the diced mango with the remaining 2 tablespoons of sugar and let stand for 2 to 3 minutes until the sugar is dissolved. Fold into the cream. In a small saucepan dissolve the gelatin in the water, then heat just until dissolved. Let cool and fold into the cream. Refrigerate.

*To make the guava cream:* Peel, seed, and coarsely chop one of the guavas and purée in a blender or food processor until smooth. Strain through a fine-mesh sieve and add 1 tablespoon of sugar. Follow the instructions for the mango cream, above, substituting guava purée and fresh guava.

*To make the chocolate ganache:* In a medium saucepan combine the chocolate, cream, and sugar. Bring to a boil over medium heat and cook, stirring constantly, until the chocolate is melted and the mixture is smooth. Let cool.

*To make the chocolate glaze:* In a double boiler over simmering water combine the chocolate, butter, rum, and corn syrup, and heat until the chocolate is melted. Stir to combine. Let cool.

*To make the toffee crunch:* Using a heavy chef's knife, coarsely chop the candy bars. Set aside.

*To assemble the meringue:* Place 1 strip of meringue on a baking sheet lined with parchment paper or waxed paper. Spread the mango cream over the layer and sprinkle with half the toffee crunch. Place a second layer of meringue on top, spread with the guava cream, and sprinkle the remaining toffee crunch on top. Place the third layer on top and cover with the ganache. Place in the refrigerator to chill until set, about 2 hours. Pour the glaze over the top. Don't worry if some runs down the sides, as the edges will be trimmed.

*To make the chocolate finish:* In a medium saucepan over simmering water melt the white chocolate. In another medium saucepan over simmering water melt the milk chocolate. Make alternate lines down the length of the meringue with the white chocolate and milk chocolate. Pull a knife through the chocolate across the width of the meringue in opposite directions, making a decorative design. Refrigerate for at least 1 hour.

*To serve:* Trim the edges, using a sharp thin-bladed knife. The piece will measure approximately 4x17 inches. Cut across the width into 12 alternating wedges about $1\frac{1}{2}$ inches wide at the widest point. Place the sauces and crème fraîche in squeeze bottles.

For each dessert plate, make concentric circles of the sauces in the order in which they are listed. Highlight the sauces with a few circles of crème fraîche. Tilt and shake the plates, twirling to make a swirled design of the sauces. Stand 1 meringue wedge upright on the wide end of each plate. Place small scoops of the sorbets to one side and garnish with fresh fruits.

# Mocha Toffee Meringue

*Kathy Cary*
LILLY'S
LOUISVILLE, KENTUCKY

**SERVES 8**

MERINGUE:

| | |
|---|---|
| 8 | egg whites |
| ½ | teaspoon cream of tartar |
| ½ | teaspoon salt |
| 2 | cups sugar |
| ½ | teaspoon vanilla extract |

MOCHA FILLING:

| | |
|---|---|
| 1 | cup sugar |
| ⅓ | cup water |
| 1 | ounce semisweet chocolate |
| 3 | egg yolks |
| 1 | tablespoon instant coffee dissolved in 1 table-spoon warm water |
| 1½ | cups (3 sticks) butter, at room temperature, cut into cubes |

CHOCOLATE MOUSSE:

| | |
|---|---|
| ¼ | pound semisweet chocolate |
| 1½ | cups heavy (whipping) cream |
| 1 | tablespoon Amaretto |

CHANTILLY:

| | |
|---|---|
| 1 | cup heavy whipping cream |
| ¼ | cup confectioners' sugar |
| ½ | teaspoon vanilla extract |

| | |
|---|---|
| | Semisweet chocolate for chocolate curls |
| | Cocoa |
| 3¾ | ounces Heath bar or homemade toffee, chopped |

✤ *To make the meringue:* Preheat the oven to 250°F. In the bowl of an electric mixer fitted with a balloon whip, combine the egg whites, cream of tartar, and salt. Whisk on high speed until soft peaks form. In a steady stream add the sugar and continue beating at high speed about 3 minutes until stiff. Add the vanilla and beat about 2 minutes until dry peaks are formed. Spoon the meringue mixture into a pastry bag and pipe 2-inch circles onto a cookie sheet that has been lined with parchment paper. Continue to spiral each circle upward to about 2½ to 3 inches, leaving the center hollow, filling only the bottom completely. Place the meringues in the preheated oven and bake 1 hour and 30 minutes until dry. Remove from the oven and cool for 45 minutes before handling.

✤ *To make the mocha filling:* In a small saucepan combine the sugar and water and cook over medium heat until the sugar dissolves. Remove the pan from the heat and let cool slightly. In the top of a double boiler over hot water melt the chocolate. Remove the chocolate from the heat and let cool. In a large bowl beat the egg yolks with a whisk until smooth. Slowly whisk in the sugar water. Continue stirring and add the coffee, chocolate, and butter. Chill in the refrigerator at least 2 hours or overnight.

*To make the chocolate mousse:* In the top of a double boiler over 1 inch of hot water melt the chocolate slowly. Remove the chocolate from the heat, stir until smooth, and let cool. Place the heavy cream in the well-chilled bowl of an electric mixer fitted with a chilled balloon whip and beat on high speed about 1 minute until peaks form. With the mixer on low speed, add the chocolate and continue mixing until the chocolate is completely incorporated. Add the Amaretto and whip until stiff. Chill this mixture 2 hours or overnight.

*To make the chantilly:* Place the whipping cream in the well-chilled bowl of an electric mixer fitted with a well-chilled balloon whip. Whip on high until cream is frothy. In a steady stream add the sugar and whip until the cream begins to form peaks. Add the vanilla and whip until stiff.

*To make chocolate curls:* With a swivel-blade scraper shave the chocolate in long strands to make curls.

*To assemble:* Sprinkle cocoa over individual serving plates. Place a meringue bowl in the center of each plate. Fill each meringue with 4 tablespoons of mocha filling, add 1 tablespoon of chopped toffee, and top with 2 tablespoons of chocolate mousse. Finally, finish the meringue by topping off with 3 tablespoons of chantilly cream. Decorate the tops of the meringues with chocolate curls.

# Chocolate Terrine

Seth Raynor
THE BOARDING HOUSE
NANTUCKET, MASSACHUSETTS

**SERVES 12**

| | | |
|---|---|---|
| 1 | pound bittersweet chocolate, shaved | Whipped cream |
| ½ | pound unsalted butter, cubed | Raspberry cookies |
| ⅔ | cup Kahlua | Chocolate sauce |
| 6 | eggs | Fresh raspberries for garnish |
| ¼ | cup sugar | Mint for garnish |

Preheat the oven to 425°F. In the top of a double boiler over simmering water melt the chocolate, butter, and Kahlua.

In a mixing bowl whisk together the eggs and sugar. Place the bowl over a pan of hot water. Whisk the mixture until the sugar is dissolved and the eggs have doubled or tripled in volume. (An electric mixer may be used if desired.) Fold the egg mixture into the chocolate mixture by thirds.

Spray twelve 4-ounce ramekins with vegetable spray. Divide mixture into ramekins. Place in a water bath (or a baking pan with enough water in it to go partway up the sides of the ramekins). Bake at 425°F uncovered for 5 minutes. Cover with foil and bake 10 minutes.

Remove from the water bath, and let cool for 45 minutes. Refrigerate for a few hours or overnight.

*To serve:* Place the ramekins in a sauté pan of hot water to reach halfway up the ramekins. Simmer briefly. Invert onto parchment-lined baking sheet. The terrines may be refrigerated at this point.

Place each terrine in the middle of a serving plate. Top with whipped cream. Decorate the plate with raspberry cookies and chocolate sauce. Garnish with fresh raspberries and mint. Sprinkle with confectioners' sugar.

# Chocolate Rum Terrine

*Carolyn Buster*
THE COTTAGE
CHICAGO, ILLINOIS

**SERVES 12 TO 15**

## TERRINE:

| | |
|---|---|
| 8 | ounces bittersweet chocolate, chopped (slightly sweetened dark chocolate available in specialty stores) |
| 1 | teaspoon Swiss coffee paste or 1 ounce chocolate mocha bean candy |
| 3 | tablespoons prepared strong coffee |
| 1 | cup (2 sticks) unsalted butter, at room temperature |
| 8 | large eggs, separated |
| ½ | cup sugar |
| ⅔ | cup all-purpose flour |
| 3 | ounces strong dark rum (Baczewski Tea-Rum, if available) |
| ½ | teaspoon salt |

## WHITE CHOCOLATE MOUSSE:

| | |
|---|---|
| 2 | envelopes (¼ ounce each) unflavored gelatin |
| 1 | cup milk |
| 1 | pound white chocolate, chopped |
| 2 | teaspoons lemon juice |
| | Zest of 2 oranges, grated and rinsed in very hot water |
| ¼ | cup Grand Marnier |
| 4 | egg whites |
| 2 | cups heavy (whipping) cream |

## MILK CHOCOLATE MOUSSE:

| | |
|---|---|
| 1 | pound milk chocolate, chopped |
| 2 | ounces prepared strong coffee |
| 4 | egg yolks |
| 2 | ounces Bailey's Irish Cream |
| 2 | teaspoons lemon juice |
| 2 | egg whites |
| 1 | cup heavy (whipping) cream |

## DARK CHOCOLATE MOUSSE:

| | |
|---|---|
| 1 | pound bittersweet chocolate, chopped |
| ½ | cup prepared strong coffee |
| 4 | egg yolks |
| ¼ | cup Tia Maria |
| 2 | egg whites |
| 1 | cup heavy (whipping) cream |

## CHOCOLATE RUM GLAZE AND SAUCE:

| | |
|---|---|
| 3 | cups sugar |
| 1 | cup good quality cocoa |
| 2 | cups water |
| 2 | to 3¾ cups (4 to 7½ sticks) butter, cut in pieces (flavor and shine increase with additional butter) |
| ½ | cup strong dark rum (Baczewski Tea-Rum, if available) |
| ¼ | cup brandy |
| ¼ | cup cognac |

*To make the terrine:* Preheat the oven to 350°F. Butter a 12x4x4-inch ovenproof terrine or 2 standard loaf pans and line the bottom with buttered waxed paper. In a saucepan combine the chocolate, coffee paste or candy, and coffee, and melt together. When smooth, whisk in the butter. In a large bowl beat the egg yolks until light and fluffy, gradually adding sugar, flour, and rum. Stir the egg yolk mixture into the melted chocolate. In a separate bowl beat the egg whites with salt until stiff. Quickly fold together the chocolate batter and beaten egg whites. Pour into the prepared terrine.

Set the terrine in a larger pan and pour hot water to reach halfway up the sides of the terrine. Bake approximately 90 minutes or until firm. Cool to room temperature. Invert; remove from the terrine and peel off the waxed paper. Chill. The terrine will keep for 1 or 2 days in the refrigerator.

    *To make the white chocolate mousse:* In a saucepan soften the gelatin in the milk. Add the white chocolate and melt together, stirring occasionally. Add the lemon juice, orange zest, and Grand Marnier. Stir over an ice water bath a few minutes to cool and firm. In a medium bowl beat the egg whites until firm and fold into the chocolate mixture. In a separate bowl whip the cream into soft peaks, and fold into the chocolate. Chill in the refrigerator.

    *To make the milk chocolate mousse:* In a saucepan combine the chocolate and coffee, and melt together, stirring occasionally. In a medium bowl beat the egg yolks until light and thick. Stir the yolks into the melted chocolate. Add the Bailey's and lemon juice. Stir the mixture over an ice water bath to cool and thicken. In a large bowl beat the egg whites until firm, and fold into the chocolate mixture. In a separate bowl whip the cream into soft peaks, and fold into the chocolate. Chill the mousse in the refrigerator.

    *To make the dark chocolate mousse:* In a saucepan combine the chocolate and coffee, and melt together, stirring occasionally. In a medium bowl beat egg yolks until light and thick. Stir the yolks into the melted chocolate, then add the Tia Maria. Stir the mixture over an ice water bath to cool and thicken. In a large bowl beat the egg whites until firm, and fold into the chocolate mixture. Whip the cream to soft peaks and fold into the chocolate. Chill the mousse in the refrigerator.

    *To make the chocolate rum glaze and sauce:* In a heavy saucepan combine the sugar, cocoa, and water. Bring to a low boil, then simmer, stirring frequently, for 10 to 15 minutes until the mixture is thick enough to coat the back of a spoon. Remove the pan from the heat and stir in the butter. Reserve 1 cup for glazing the terrine. Add the rum, brandy, and cognac to the remaining chocolate mixture. Let cool to room temperature.

Pour the reserved glaze over the terrine. On each serving plate place 1 slice of terrine and surround with a scoop of each of the three mousses. Ladle chocolate sauce on the plate to surround the terrine and mousses. Garnish with fresh strawberries, mint leaves, and whipped cream, if desired.

# Milk Chocolate Caramel Crème Brûlée

*Kate Chorlton*
PARK AVENUE CAFE
NEW YORK, NEW YORK

## MAKES 24 2-INCH RAMEKINS OR 12 4-INCH RAMEKINS

MILK CHOCOLATE CARAMEL CRÈME
BRÛLÉE:

3   cups milk
2¾   cups cream
⅓   cup sugar
½   cup water
¾   cup sugar

12   ounces chocolate, chopped
8   egg yolks

SUGAR GLAZE:

½   cup light brown sugar
½   cup pure cane sugar

✎ *To make the milk chocolate caramel crème brûlée:* In a saucepan bring to a boil the milk, cream, and ⅓ cup of sugar.

In another saucepan cook the water and ¾ cup of sugar to an amber color.

Slowly pour and blend one-third of the milk carefully into the caramel, then pour all back into the milk. Boil again. Pour the mixture over the chopped chocolate in a bowl. Cool to room temperature. Add the yolks and stir together. Strain the mixture.

Preheat the oven to 325°F. Pour the custard into shallow brûlée-type dishes. Bake in a water bath for about 35 minutes or until the custard sets. Remove from the water bath and let cool.

✎ *To make the sugar glaze:* Mix together the light brown sugar and pure cane sugar. Sprinkle the custards with the sugar mixture and glaze under the broiler (or with a torch) before serving.

# Chocolate Crème Brûlée with a Sweet Basil Vanilla Sauce

*Peter deJong*
THE BEAUFORT INN
BEAUFORT, SOUTH CAROLINA

**SERVES 4**

CHOCOLATE CRÈME BRÛLÉE:

| | |
|---|---|
| 5 | ounces bitter chocolate |
| ½ | cup heavy (whipping) cream |
| 3 | large eggs |
| ¾ | cup sugar |
| 1½ | cups milk |

SWEET BASIL VANILLA SAUCE:

| | |
|---|---|
| ½ | cup milk |
| 1 | cup basil leaves |
| ¼ | cup sugar |

| | |
|---|---|
| 1 | cup heavy (whipping) cream |
| 1 | vanilla bean |

DARK AND WHITE CHOCOLATE TRIANGLES:

| | |
|---|---|
| 4 | ounces white chocolate |
| 4 | ounces semisweet chocolate |

| | |
|---|---|
| ¼ | cup firmly packed light brown sugar |
| ½ | cup fresh raspberries |

*To prepare the crème brûlée:* Preheat the oven to 300°F. Place the chocolate in a small metal bowl. In a heavy saucepan heat the cream over moderately high heat until it just comes to a boil and pour over the chocolate. Let the chocolate stand until softened and whisk the mixture until smooth. In a separate bowl whisk together the eggs and sugar. Whisk in the chocolate mixture. In a saucepan heat the milk just to a boil. Add the milk to the egg mixture in a stream, whisking. Skim off any froth. Divide the custard among four ½-cup flameproof ramekins set in a roasting pan. Add enough hot water to the pan to reach halfway up the sides of the ramekins. Bake the custards in the middle of the oven about 60 minutes until they are just set but still tremble slightly. Remove the ramekins.

*To prepare the basil vanilla sauce:* In the bowl of a food processor combine the milk, basil, and sugar, and purée until smooth. In a small heavy saucepan bring the puréed mixture just to a boil with the cream and vanilla bean. Remove the pan from the heat. Scrape the seeds from the vanilla bean with a knife into the pan, reserving the pod for another use. Cover and refrigerate for at least 2 hours.

*To prepare the chocolate triangles:* Line a 10x15-inch cookie sheet with parchment paper. Temper the white chocolate: In the bottom of a double boiler heat 1 inch of water over medium heat. Place 4 ounces of white chocolate in the top of the double boiler and heat, stirring constantly, for about 3 minutes or until the chocolate has melted. Transfer the melted chocolate to a stainless steel bowl and continue stirring until the mixture is cooled. Temper the dark chocolate using the same procedure as for the white chocolate. Pour the white and dark chocolate side by side on the parchment paper. Use a rubber spatula to evenly spread the chocolates (making sure to keep the chocolates separate). Place the baking sheet in the refrigerator until the chocolate has set, about 10 minutes. Remove from the refrigerator and invert the chocolate onto a cutting board. Cut the chocolates into triangles.

*To assemble:* Set broiler rack so that custards will be 2 to 3 inches from heat and preheat broiler. Sift brown sugar evenly over custards and broil custards until sugar is melted and caramelized, about 2 minutes. (Alternately, raw sugar may be sprinkled over the custards and caramelized with a blowtorch.) Place brûlées on individual dessert plates and surround with the sauce, a white and a dark chocolate triangle, and fresh raspberries.

*Pecan Profiteroles with Vanilla Ice Cream, Chocolate Sauce, and Seasonal Fruit*

*Honey and Hawaiian Vintage Chocolate Ganache*

*Chocolate Layered Lime Parfait with Raspberry Coulis*

*Dentelle Croustillante*

*Chocolate-Raspberry Tamales with White Chocolate Ice Cream*

*Swans with White Chocolate Mousse*

*White Chocolate Mango Mousse*

*White Chocolate Mousse Cake*

# Chocolate Pâté

Joyce Banister
BISTRO LA TOUR
NEW ORLEANS, LOUISIANA

**SERVES 8**

Delightfully decadent describes chef Joyce Banister's Chocolate Pâté, especially when it is served, as Banister suggests, with a small glass of a nice, full-bodied, Cabernet Sauvignon.

2   *pounds bittersweet chocolate, preferably Callebaut, chopped, plus ½ pound chopped*
1½  *cups (3 sticks) sweet butter, cut into 1-inch pieces*

½   *cup Chambord (raspberry liqueur)*
1   *cup water*
4   *egg yolks, beaten*

*To make the chocolate pâté:* Line a small loaf pan with plastic wrap to form a mold.

In a double boiler over barely simmering water melt 2 pounds of the chocolate with the butter, Chambord, and water, stirring until smooth. Set aside and let cool slightly.

Whisk the egg yolks into the chocolate mixture. Strain through a fine mesh sieve into the prepared mold, cover, and chill.

*To serve:* In a double boiler over barely simmering water melt the remaining ½ pound of chocolate, stirring until smooth.

Dip a large knife into hot water and cut the pâté into 1-inch slices. Decorate each serving plate with swirls of melted chocolate. Place a slice of pâté on each plate and serve.

# Lemon Cream Cappuccino

*Jeff Walters*
LA MER, HALEKULANI HOTEL
HONOLULU, OAHU

**SERVES 6**

It helps to have a cool kitchen and cool hands when you create chocolate pieces like these little cups. Once you have mastered them, the cups can be used to hold a variety of fillings. Here they are used to present coffee-flavored sabayon and tart lemon cream. The cups, lemon cream, and sabayon should all be made 1 day ahead. You can simplify the preparation by substituting pieces of ladyfinger or sponge cake for the bisquit. You'll find the mocha paste at bakers' supply stores.

CHOCOLATE CUPS:

4    ounces couverture chocolate

LEMON CREAM:

4    whole eggs
1    cup sugar
1    cup (2 sticks) unsalted butter at room temperature, cut into pieces
     Grated zest and juice of 4 lemons

CAPPUCCINO SABAYON:

3    egg yolks
¼    cup sugar
½    envelope plain gelatin

½    cup brewed cold decaffeinated espresso
¼    cup Kahlua
1    tablespoon mocha paste
1¼   cups heavy (whipping) cream

ST. MARC BISQUIT:

¾    cup almonds
2    tablespoons sugar
11   egg whites
⅞    cup plus 1¼ cups sugar
1    cup cake flour
¼    cup brewed cold decaffeinated espresso
⅓    cup heavy (whipping) cream
     Cocoa for dusting

*To make the cups:* Cut 6 heavy, flexible plastic strips 8¾ inches long and 4 inches wide. In a double boiler over simmering water, melt the chocolate and heat to 100°F. Let the chocolate cool to 90°F and place on a heating pad set on low to maintain that temperature. Lay the strips on a work surface and use a brush or thin spatula to spread a layer of chocolate less than ⅛ inch thick on a strip. When the chocolate has firmed slightly but before it is hard, lift the strip with both hands and curve it, chocolate side in, to fit inside a 3-inch ring mold or PVC pipe ring. Slip the strip inside the mold, making sure the ends of the strip just meet. Repeat with the remainder of the strips. Roll 1 tablespoon chocolate between your palms and the work surface until it forms a 10-inch long stick. Make 6; refrigerate to set.

Lay a piece of parchment or waxed paper on a work surface and spread a layer of chocolate ⅛ inch thick or less on the paper. Let set until firm, then lay a second layer of paper over the chocolate, grasp both layers of paper, and flip the entire stack. Remove the first layer of paper, exposing a smooth chocolate surface. Using a 3½-inch diameter glass or ring mold, cut through the chocolate with the point of a sharp knife to make six 3½-inch diameter circles. Pull the remaining chocolate away from the circles and set aside.

When the chocolate molds are completely set, lift the plastic circles out of the ring molds and gently peel off the plastic strips, exposing the chocolate cylinders. Lift the chocolate disks from the parchment and place 1 on each serving plate. Warm a sheet pan in a 200°F oven. Put the warm pan on a work surface. With cool hands, gently lift one of the chocolate cylinders, touch one end of it briefly to the warmed pan until it starts to melt, then place immediately in the center of one of the chocolate circles, forming a cup. Repeat with the remaining cylinders. Place in the refrigerator or freezer until set, or store overnight.

*To make the lemon cream:* In a large bowl beat the eggs and sugar together until smooth. Add the butter and zest and beat until smooth again. Put in a double boiler over barely simmering water and cook until the mixture thickens, about 12 minutes, stirring constantly. Stir in the lemon juice and cook for 2 to 3 more minutes, stirring constantly. Remove from heat and let cool slightly until it begins to set. Strain through a fine-mesh sieve into a bowl, cover, and refrigerate overnight.

*To make the sabayon:* In a double boiler over barely simmering water combine the egg yolks and sugar until it gets thick and foamy, about 1 minute. Sprinkle the gelatin over the espresso. Stir in the Kahlua and mocha paste. Stir in the mixture into the sabayon and place the pan in a bowl of ice water to chill, stirring occasionally. In a deep bowl beat the cream until soft peaks form and gently fold in the sabayon, blending well. Cover and refrigerate overnight.

*To make the bisquit:* In a food processor or nut grinder combine the almonds and sugar and process to a fine meal. In a large bowl beat the egg whites and the ⅞ cup of sugar until stiff peaks form. Sift the almond meal, remaining sugar, and cake flour and gently fold into the meringue.

Preheat the oven to 400°F. Line one half of a jelly roll pan with parchment or waxed paper and spray with vegetable oil cooking spray. Spread the mixture evenly over the paper and bake for 5 to 7 minutes, until firm. Let cool and cut into 2½-inch circles to fit inside the chocolate cups.

*To serve:* Remove the cups, lemon cream, and sabayon from the refrigerator. Whip the lemon cream and the sabayon to restore their light texture. With an iced tea spoon or similar small spoon, place a dot of lemon cream in the bottom of each cup to anchor the bisquit. Gently press a bisquit circle inside the cup and soak it with 2 teaspoons of espresso. Spoon in more lemon cream until the cup is half filled, then fill to within ⅛ inch of the top with the cappuccino sabayon. Repeat with the remaining cups. In a deep bowl whip the cream until it just starts to thicken. Spoon the cream over the sabayon to the top of each cup. Garnish each cup with a chocolate stick and dust the cup and plate with cocoa.

# Honey and Hawaiian Vintage Chocolate Ganache with Gold-Dusted Chocolate Leaves and Poha Berry Sauce

*Philippe Padovani*

THE MANELE BAY HOTEL
LANAI CITY, LANAI

**SERVES 4**

This rich-as-Croesus dessert combines the melting texture and taste of honey ganache with bittersweet chocolate frills garnished with gold leaf. The slightly tart sauce provides counterpoint to the richness of the chocolate. It can, of course, be made without the touch of gold; sprinkle just a little confectioners' sugar on each frill if you prefer.

**KIAWE HONEY GANACHE:**

¼  cup heavy (whipping) cream
½  Polynesian or other vanilla bean, halved
       lengthwise
2  tablespoons Kiawe or other fragrant honey
2  ounces Hawaiian vintage or other fine-quality
       bittersweet chocolate, chopped
2  tablespoons unsalted butter

**POHA BERRY SAUCE:**

1  cup milk
½  Polynesian or other vanilla bean, split length-
       wise

3  egg yolks
¼  cup sugar
1  cup fresh poha berries or Cape Gooseberries
       or raspberries

**CHOCOLATE LEAVES:**

9  ounces Hawaiian Vintage or other high-
       quality bittersweet chocolate
2  tablespoons canola or other light vegetable oil
2  sheets gold leaf (optional), or confectioners'
       sugar for dusting

*To make the ganache:* In a heavy saucepan bring the cream to a boil over medium-high heat. Add the vanilla bean and honey. Set aside for 15 minutes to infuse flavors. Remove the vanilla bean and add the chocolate, stirring until the chocolate has melted and the ganache is smooth. Pour into a small bowl and stir in the butter. Set aside and let cool.

*To make the sauce:* In a medium saucepan bring the milk to a boil over medium high heat and add the vanilla bean. Set aside for 15 minutes to infuse the flavors. Remove the vanilla bean. In a medium bowl combine the egg yolks and sugar and whisk until smooth. Pour the hot milk over the mixture, stirring constantly. Pour the egg mixture into the pan and cook over medium heat, stirring constantly, until the sauce is thick enough to coat the spoon. Be careful not to let it boil. Place the berries or raspberries in a medium bowl and strain the sauce through a fine-mesh sieve into the bowl over the berries. With a mixer, blend until smooth. Place the bowl in a bowl of ice water to chill the sauce quickly. Cover and refrigerate.

✍ *To make the chocolate leaves:* In a double boiler over simmering water melt the chocolate and heat to 100°F. Add the oil to the chocolate and blend well. Let cool to 90°F. Using 2 ungreased jelly roll pans, pour half of the melted chocolate evenly over the surface of each pan, spread it out, and let cool completely. With a spatula, putty knife, or your thumbnail, scrape the chocolate off the pan in 1½-inch frilled strips and pinch the loose piece at one end for a leaflike design. Make 6 leaves for each plate. Using the point of a knife, with very light strokes, brush off the gold from the back of half of a gold sheet until the gold attaches to the chocolate. Set aside.

✍ *To serve:* Use 4 chilled dessert plates. Fill a pastry bag with the ganache and pipe 5 dots about 1 inch in diameter near the edge of each plate. Attach 1 leaf per dot in a pleasing pattern. If using confectioners' sugar instead of gold, dust with confectioners' sugar. Divide the sauce among the plates and pour a border of sauce around each leaf pattern.

# Frozen Lime Ganache Parfait with Chocolate Tuiles

Christopher Malta
1848 HOUSE
ATLANTA, GEORGIA

**SERVES 6**

Silky-smooth ganache centers put a touch of surprise in smooth, frozen lime parfaits. Fruit sauces add color and bright flavor notes. Begin a day ahead to allow time for freezing.

GANACHE:

| | |
|---|---|
| 1 | cup heavy (whipping) cream |
| 2 | tablespoons unsalted butter |
| 2 | tablespoons sugar |
| 12 | ounces bittersweet chocolate, chopped |

LIME PARFAIT:

| | |
|---|---|
| 1 | envelope unflavored gelatin |
| 2 | tablespoons cold water |
| 3 | egg yolks |
| 2 | tablespoons cornstarch |
| 1/3 | cup heavy (whipping) cream |
| 1/3 | cup sugar |
| | Juice of 4 large fresh limes (about 2/3 cup) |
| 3 | egg whites |
| 1/4 | cup sugar |

CHOCOLATE TUILES:

*(Makes 24 to 30 medium cookies)*

| | |
|---|---|
| 3/4 | cup (1½ sticks) unsalted butter |
| 2 | cups sugar |
| 6 | egg whites |
| 1/4 | teaspoon vanilla extract |
| 2 | cups all-purpose flour |
| 1 | cup cocoa |

GARNISH:

| | |
|---|---|
| 1 | cup Peach Sauce (page 187) |
| 1 | cup Strawberry Sauce (page 187) |
| 1 | cup Kiwi Sauce (page 187) |
| 1 | cup Crème Anglaise (page 189) |
| 6 | pansies |
| 2 | sprigs fresh mint |
| | Chocolate Tuiles |

☙ *To make the ganache:* In a deep, heavy pan stir together the cream, butter, and sugar and bring to a boil over medium-high heat. Remove the pan from the heat and add the chocolate. Let sit for 5 minutes, then stir to blend. Cover and refrigerate until chilled. Reserving 1 cup for garnish, roll the ganache between your hands to form six walnut-size balls. Refrigerate.

☙ *To make the parfait:* Soften the gelatin in the water. In the top of a double boiler or a medium metal bowl whisk together the egg yolks and cornstarch until the cornstarch is absorbed. In a deep, heavy pan over low heat stir the cream and sugar together until the sugar is dissolved. Whisking constantly, slowly pour the cream mixture into the eggs and cornstarch. Place over a double boiler with simmering water and whisk gently for 3 to 4 minutes until thickened. Whisk in the lime juice and the softened gelatin, whisking until the gelatin is completely melted and dissolved in the custard. Remove the pan from the heat and place the pan or bowl in a large bowl of ice water to cool. In a deep bowl beat the egg whites and sugar until soft peaks form. Add the egg whites all at once to the cooled lime custard and fold until blended; the egg whites will lose about half their volume. Fill six 3x2-inch round molds three-quarters full with the lime parfait mixture, and press a ganache ball into the center of each. Finish filling the molds with the parfait mixture, and smooth with the back of a spoon to seal. Freeze for at least 3 hours or overnight.

*To make the chocolate tuiles:* Preheat the oven to 350°F. Using an Xacto-type blade or razor, cut a pleasing design in a thin plastic lid of the type that covers tubs of butter. Line a baking pan with parchment paper. In the large bowl of a mixer or a food processor cream the butter and sugar. Slowly beat in the egg whites. Add the vanilla. Stir in the flour until blended. Add the cocoa and stir until the color is uniform.

Place the stencil on the parchment paper and spread the batter over the stencil. Lift and repeat to use all of the batter. Bake 10 minutes or until the tuiles are semi-firm. Remove from the oven and immediately lift the tuiles with a spatula, placing them over a rolling pin or bottles to mold them.

*To serve:* Prepare the dessert plates. Warm the reserved ganache until liquefied and place it in a squeeze bottle. Draw a multi-petaled flower or other pleasing design on each plate with the ganache. Place each fruit sauce and the crème anglaise in a separate squeeze bottle. Fill in the "petals" of the design with a mosaic of different colored fruit sauces, ending with a center of crème Anglaise.

Dip each mold up to the rim in warm water for 5 to 7 seconds to loosen, then unmold onto a large plate or platter. Cut through about one-quarter of one parfait. Place both pieces on one of the serving plates, separating the pieces to reveal the ganache center. Garnish with a pansy and mint leaves. Repeat with the remaining molds.

# Helter Skelter Parfait

Shane Gorringe
WINDSOR COURT HOTEL
NEW ORLEANS, LOUISIANA

**SERVES 6**

The three flavors and colors of this layered sorbet parfait make a beautiful dessert. If making chocolate ornaments isn't your cup of tea, melt only 3 ounces of chocolate for the parfait mixture, and substitute chocolate curls or shaved chocolate for the lattices to be made from the remaining chocolate.

PARFAIT:

| | |
|---|---|
| 8 | egg yolks |
| 1 | cup sugar |
| ¼ | cup water |
| 3 | ounces chopped bittersweet chocolate |
| 6 | cups heavy (whipping) cream |
| 3 | tablespoons Framboise liqueur |
| ½ | cup raspberries |

MARINATED RASPBERRIES AND SAUCE:

| | |
|---|---|
| 2 | cups raspberries |
| ¾ | cup crème de cacao |
| ¼ | cup sugar |

CHOCOLATE GARNISH:

| | |
|---|---|
| 2 | ounces semisweet chocolate |

&#x276f; *To make the parfait:* Place the egg yolks in a medium mixing bowl. In a small saucepan combine the sugar and water, stir together, and bring to a boil over medium heat. When the sugar reaches 245°F or soft ball stage (a small amount dropped from a spoon into cold water will form a soft ball), pour it over the yolks while mixing at medium speed. When all the sugar is added, increase the speed to high. Continue whipping until the mixture is cool. Divide this mixture between two bowls and set aside.

In a double boiler over barely simmering water, melt the chocolate, stirring until smooth; set aside.

In a large, deep bowl beat the heavy cream until soft peaks form. To the first bowl of reserved egg mixture fold in half of the whipped cream and 2 tablespoons of Framboise. Set aside.

To the second bowl of reserved mixture fold in the remaining whipped cream, 1 tablespoon of Framboise, and the melted chocolate. Pipe or spoon alternating layers of the two mixtures into each of six 6-ounce parfait glasses or tumblers, placing a few raspberries between each layer. Freeze for 8 to 10 hours.

&#x276f; *To make the berries and sauce:* Combine the raspberries and crème de cacao and let sit at room temperature for 3 to 4 hours. Drain the crème de cacao from the berries into a small saucepan, reserving the berries for later. Add the sugar to the crème de cacao and bring to a boil over medium heat for 4 to 5 minutes. Let cool. Put the raspberries back into the sauce.

Unmold the parfaits by dipping them up to the rim in a pan of warm water for 5 to 10 seconds, and then turning them onto a plate. The parfaits should slide out; if not, return them to the warm water and turn them over again. Place the parfaits on a tray and return them to the freezer for 5 to 10 hours.

*To make the chocolate garnish:* Cut 6 strips of baking parchment about 14 inches long and 3 inches wide. Melt the semisweet chocolate in a double boiler over barely simmering water, and put it in a pastry bag fitted with a ¼-inch tip. Pipe a chocolate lattice design the length of each strip. Before the chocolate sets, wrap a strip around each parfait. Freeze.

*To serve:* Unwrap the paper from the chocolate. (If the chocolate gets too soft, place the lattices in the freezer for a few minutes to reset.) Garnish with berries and sauce.

# Pecan Profiteroles with Vanilla Ice Cream, Chocolate Sauce, and Seasonal Fruit

*Daphne Macias*
PELICAN CLUB
NEW ORLEANS, LOUISIANA

## MAKES 24 PROFITEROLES; 8 SERVINGS OF 3 PROFITEROLES PER SERVING

Chef Daphne Macias adds pecans and fresh fruit to a classic French dessert: cream puffs filled with ice cream and topped with chocolate sauce.

PÂTE À CHOUX:

| | |
|---|---|
| ½ | cup milk |
| ½ | cup water |
| ½ | cup (1 stick) butter |
| 1 | cup all-purpose flour |
| 2 | tablespoons sugar |
| 4 | eggs |

CHOCOLATE SAUCE:

| | |
|---|---|
| 2 | cups heavy (whipping) cream |
| 1 | cup packed brown sugar |
| 1 | pound chocolate, chopped |
| | *Vanilla ice cream* |
| 2 | tablespoons ground pecans |
| | *Mixed fresh blackberries, raspberries, and sliced hulled strawberries* |

*To make the pâte a choux:* Preheat the oven to 400°F. Line 2 baking sheets with parchment. In a medium saucepan combine the milk, water, and butter, and bring to a boil over medium-high heat. Add the flour and sugar all at once, and stir the mixture until it forms a ball and comes away from the side of the pan, about 2 or 3 minutes. Add the eggs one at a time, stirring until each is blended. Remove from the heat and let stand for 5 minutes. Place the mixture in a pastry bag with a 1-inch plain tip. Pipe 24 portions 2 inches apart on the prepared pans. Bake for 10 minutes, then reduce the heat to 350°F and bake for 10 to 15 minutes or until light brown.

*To make the chocolate sauce:* In a medium saucepan combine the heavy cream and brown sugar and bring to a boil over medium-high heat. Turn off the heat. Stir in the chocolate pieces until melted and blended. Keep warm.

Using a 2-ounce ice cream scoop, make 24 scoops of ice cream and place them on a waxed paper lined tray. Place in the freezer.

*To serve:* Cut the profiteroles in half crosswise. Fill each with a scoop of ice cream and cover with the top. Serve 3 profiteroles per serving. Ladle 1 tablespoon of chocolate sauce over each profiterole. Garnish with pecans and fresh fruit.

# Chocolate-Laced Praline Shells with Berries and Amaretto Cream

## Andrea Tritico

BELLA LUNA
NEW ORLEANS, LOUISIANA

**MAKES ABOUT 18 SHELLS; SERVES 18**

This make-ahead recipe can be assembled right before serving. Make the batter for the praline shells two days before serving, and make the shells themselves the day before. Coat the insides of the shells with chocolate. Fill the coated shells with fresh berries and top with amaretto cream just before serving.

PRALINE SHELLS:

½   cup (1 stick) butter
1½   cups packed brown sugar
1   cup corn syrup
2   cups all-purpose flour

AMARETTO CREAM:

2   cups sour cream
⅓   cup packed brown sugar
¼   cup Amaretto liqueur

1   pound semisweet chocolate, chopped
2   cups fresh strawberries, hulled and quartered
2   cups fresh raspberries

*To make the praline shells:* In a large saucepan combine the butter, sugar, and corn syrup, and bring to a boil over medium heat. Place the flour in a large bowl and pour in the hot mixture. Stir until well mixed. Cover and chill overnight.

Preheat the oven to 350°F. Divide the batter into 1½-tablespoon portions and roll into balls. Place the balls on a baking sheet lined with baking parchment, leaving at least 5 inches of space between each one. Bake until golden in the center and darker brown around the edges.

Remove the entire parchment paper from the pan and place on a cool working surface. With one quick motion, turn the paper over, leaving the shells on the surface. Pick up the shells and one by one drape them over a teacup or custard cup. This entire process should be completed as quickly as possible. Let cool.

*To make the Amaretto cream:* In a small bowl combine the sour cream, brown sugar, and Amaretto, and mix until thoroughly blended; set aside. When the shells have set and completely cooled, melt the chocolate in a double boiler over barely simmering water, stirring until smooth. Using a pastry brush, coat the inside of each shell with a thin layer of chocolate. Let sit for about 10 minutes or until hardened. Combine the strawberries and raspberries. Divide the berries among the shells and pour Amaretto cream over them.

# Dentelle Croustillante

Daniel Bonnot

CHEZ DANIEL
NEW ORLEANS, LOUISIANA

**SERVES 6**

The name means "lacy cookie," but it only partly describes these chocolate wafers, which are filled with pistachio cream and served in a sea of chocolate sauce.

CHOCOLATE COOKIES:

½   cup sugar
½   cup firmly packed brown sugar
1   cup unsweetened cocoa
6   tablespoons unsalted butter, at room temperature
1   cup plus 1½ tablespoons unbleached all-purpose flour
½   cup fresh orange juice
2   tablespoons dark rum

PISTACHIO CREAM:

2   cups heavy (whipping) cream
1   tablespoon confectioners' sugar, sifted
3   rounded tablespoons pistachio paste

Chocolate Ganache (page 185)

GARNISH:

8   fresh strawberries, cut into fans
3   tablespoons pistachio nuts, chopped
18   fresh mint leaves, cut into shreds
4   fresh mint sprigs
    Sifted confectioners' sugar for dusting

❧ *To make the chocolate cookies:* Preheat the oven to 375°F. In a large bowl combine the granulated and brown sugars. Add the cocoa and butter and beat together vigorously with a wooden spoon for 1 to 2 minutes. Add 1 cup of flour and stir in. The batter will be stiff. Add the orange juice and rum, and mix until smooth.

Dust a baking sheet with 1½ tablespoons of flour. Spoon about 2 tablespoons of batter per dollop onto the pan, alternating the dollops of batter so that 12 will fit on the pan with at least 3 inches of space between them. Using a rubber spatula, spread each dollop out to a 3½-inch circle. Bake for 10 minutes. Let cool completely, then cut a circle out of each cookie with a 3-inch ring mold or cookie cutter.

❧ *To make the pistachio cream:* In a deep bowl whip the cream with the sugar until soft peaks begin to form. Add the pistachio paste and beat for 1 or 2 minutes or until stiff peaks form. Transfer the cream to a pastry bag fitted with a ½-inch star tip and refrigerate.

❧ *To serve:* Spoon chocolate ganache in the center of each of 6 dessert plates and place a chocolate cookie in the center of each. Pipe rosettes of the pistachio cream over the cookie. Top with another cookie and pipe cream on top. Garnish each plate with 2 fanned strawberries. Sprinkle the pistachios and shredded mint around each plate. Garnish with mint sprigs and dust the plates with confectioners' sugar.

# Chocolate Layered Lime Parfait with Raspberry Coulis

*Josef Teuschler*
FOUR SEASONS
NEVIS

## SERVES 4

LIME PARFAIT:

| | |
|---|---|
| 1 | cup sugar |
| 7 | ounces milk |
| 12 | egg yolks |
| 1 | cup lime juice |
| | Zest of 1 lime |
| 4 | cups whipped cream |

RASPBERRY COULIS:

| | |
|---|---|
| 1 | cup fresh raspberries |
| 2 | ounces confectioners' sugar |
| | Juice of 1 lemon |

Chocolate Disks (page 183)
Shaved white chocolate

*To make the lime parfait:* Prepare a bain marie by heating a large shallow pan of water. In a saucepan combine the sugar, milk, egg yolks, lime juice, and lime zest. Place the saucepan in the bain marie and heat until slightly thickened. Remove the pan and place over a pan of ice until chilled. Fold in the whipped cream. Freeze for 3 hours.

*To make the raspberry coulis:* In a blender combine the raspberries, confectioners' sugar, and lemon juice. Blend well. Strain.

*To assemble the dessert:* Cut 3-inch disks out of chocolate. Cut 2-inch disks out of chilled lime parfait. Pour raspberry coulis on a dessert plate. Place a disk of lime parfait off center on the plate. Top with a chocolate disk. Repeat to make 4 layers of parfait and 3 layers of chocolate, ending with parfait (like a napoleon). Decorate with raspberries.

# Chocolate-Raspberry Tamales with White Chocolate Ice Cream

Royal Dahlstrom

FRANKLIN STREET BAKERY
MINNEAPOLIS, MINNESOTA

**MAKES 20 TAMALES**

FUDGE SAUCE:

1 cup heavy (whipping) cream
1½ cups light corn syrup
¼ cup (½ stick) butter
4 ounces high quality unsweetened chocolate, chopped
1¾ cups sugar
½ cup Dutch cocoa
½ cup warm water

CHOCOLATE-RASPBERRY TAMALES:

2 cups firmly packed brown sugar
2 cups (4 sticks) butter
8 eggs
3½ cups all-purpose flour
1 cup cocoa

2 teaspoons baking soda
1 teaspoon salt
½ cup warm water
1 bundle tamale skins (available at Latin American stores)
3 pints raspberries
1 quart Fudge Sauce
1 quart White Chocolate Ice Cream

WHITE CHOCOLATE ICE CREAM:

12 egg yolks
3 cups milk
1½ cups sugar
½ vanilla bean
6 ounces high quality white chocolate, chopped

To make the fudge sauce: In a saucepan heat the cream, corn syrup, and butter until the butter is melted. Add the chocolate and stir until smooth. Add the sugar and cocoa, and cook until smooth. Store in a covered container. Makes 2 quarts.

To make the chocolate-raspberry tamales: In a small electric mixer cream the brown sugar and butter together until smooth. Scrape the bowl and slowly add the eggs one at a time. In a separate bowl sift together the flour, cocoa, baking soda, and salt. Slowly add the flour mixture to the eggs. Add the butter–brown sugar mixture and blend until smooth. When the mixture thickens, slowly add the warm water.

Spread out 2 corn husks and place a dollop of cake batter on one. Place a few raspberries on the cake batter. Top with a little fudge sauce. Tear 20 strips ⅛ inch wide from 2 of the husks for tying the tamales. Place 2 husks together with the large end overlapping by 2 inches. Repeat for the remaining husks (20 set-ups), then set them up like the first setup, always leaving 1 inch at each end uncovered. Pull the corn husks so the dough filling is completely enclosed. Twist and tie each end with a strip.

Steam the tamales in a conventional steamer or vegetable basket set inside a saucepan, covered with a tight-fitting lid. It is important that little or no steam escapes while cooking. Steam for about 20 minutes, with the water always lightly boiling. The tamales are done when the dough comes away easily from the husk.

When the tamales are cooked, slice them from end to end with a knife. Push the ends gently together (as you would to widen the opening of a baked potato), transfer to serving plates, and garnish with hot fudge sauce and fresh raspberries or any kind of fruit sauce.

*To make the white chocolate ice cream:* In a mixer or by hand whip the yolks until they are light yellow and frothy. In a heavy saucepan heat the milk and sugar, stirring gently. Split and scrape the vanilla bean into the milk. Add the white chocolate and heat until melted. Scald the mixture. Slowly add one cup of hot mixture to the egg yolks, taking care not to add too fast or the yolks will scramble. Whisk together and place on a double boiler. Cook slowly until the mixture is thick enough to coat the back of a spoon. Place the pan over ice and chill.

Add the heavy cream, mix well, and strain. After the mixture cools, place in an ice cream freezer and freeze according to the manufacturer's directions.

# Marble Fudge Brownies

*Michael Romano*

UNION SQUARE CAFE
NEW YORK, NEW YORK

**SERVES 4**

The best brownies are dense, rich, and loaded with chocolate. These fit the bill perfectly, and the swirl of cream cheese adds a visual and flavor contrast to the chocolate.

2    tablespoons unsweetened cocoa for dusting

**FUDGE MIXTURE:**

9    tablespoons unsalted butter
4    ounces good-quality semisweet chocolate, chopped
2    eggs
¾    cup plus 1 tablespoon sugar
½    cup all-purpose flour
    Pinch salt

**CREAM CHEESE MIXTURE:**

1    8-ounce package of cream cheese, at room temperature
¼    cup sugar
½    teaspoon vanilla extract
1    egg

Chocolate sauce and ice cream for serving, or confectioners' sugar for dusting

*To make the fudge mixture:* Preheat the oven to 350°F. Butter four 4x1-inch round molds and dust with the cocoa. In a double boiler over barely simmering water melt the butter and chocolate, stirring to combine thoroughly. Set aside to cool slightly.

In a medium bowl whisk together the eggs and sugar until well combined. Add the chocolate mixture and stir well to incorporate. Stir in the flour and salt until blended, but do not overmix.

*To make the cream cheese mixture:* In a medium bowl beat the cream cheese and sugar until well blended. Add the vanilla and egg and continue to beat until smooth.

Fill the prepared molds three-fourths full with the chocolate mixture, then top off with cream cheese. Using a fork, swirl the layers 2 or 3 times, using a folding motion. Be careful not to over-mix or to scrape the sides or bottom of the pan, or the brownies could stick.

Bake the brownies for 35 minutes or until the tops are golden and the centers are somewhat firm. Let cool on a wire rack and unmold. Serve with chocolate sauce and your favorite ice cream, or dust with confectioners' sugar.

*Note:* The brownies may be made 1 day in advance and kept at room temperature, tightly covered with plastic wrap.

# Chocolate Coconut with Vanilla English Cream

*Kim Kringlie*
THE DAKOTA
COVINGTON, LOUISIANA

### SERVES 4

Chef Kim Kringlie's recipe is a lesson in trompe l'oeil. He dips mylar balloons into chocolate halfway up, refrigerates them to harden the chocolate, and then pops the balloons. Voilà! A hollow chocolate half sphere ready to fill. Once the cream freezes, a melon baller is used to hollow out the center to resemble the interior of a coconut half. This chocolate molding technique can be used with other fillings such as chocolate mousse, ice cream, and fresh berries drizzled with sabayon.

CHOCOLATE COCONUTS:

| | |
|---|---|
| 8 | ounces milk chocolate, chopped |
| ¼ | cup macadamia nuts, finely chopped |
| 8 | ounces cream cheese at room temperature |
| 1 | cup sifted confectioners' sugar |
| ¼ | cup coconut cream |
| 1 | cup heavy (whipping) cream |
| ¼ | cup shredded coconut |

ENGLISH CREAM:

(Makes 2 cups)

| | |
|---|---|
| ¾ | cup heavy (whipping) cream |
| ½ | cup milk |
| 4 | egg yolks |
| ½ | cup sugar |
| 2 | tablespoons pure vanilla extract |

*To make the chocolate coconuts:* Blow up Mylar balloons to a 2½-inch diameter; set aside. In a double boiler over barely simmering water melt the chocolate. Add the macadamia nuts. Dip each balloon halfway into the chocolate and refrigerate on a tray until the chocolate is firm.

In a large bowl beat the cream cheese, sugar, and coconut cream until smooth. In a deep, medium bowl whip the heavy cream until stiff peaks form. Fold the whipped cream into the cream cheese mixture and add the shredded coconut.

Pop the balloons and remove them from the chocolate shells. Fill the chocolate shells to the top with the filling. Place in the freezer until firm. Using a melon baller, hollow out the middle of the shell to resemble a coconut half. Serve with English cream.

*To make the English cream:* In a medium saucepan heat the heavy cream and milk. In a medium bowl beat the egg yolks and sugar until pale in color. Gradually beat in the hot milk and cream. Return to the saucepan and cook over medium heat, stirring constantly, until the mixture coats the back of a spoon. Add the vanilla and strain through a fine-mesh sieve.

# Kathleen's Low-Fat Chocolate Chip Ice Cream Sandwich

*Kathleen Daelemans*

CAFE KULA, GRAND WAILEA RESORT
WAILEA, MAUI

**MAKES 8 COOKIES, SERVES 4**

Hard to believe, but each of these cookies has only 2 grams of fat. Sucanot, which is evaporated cane juice, gives a distinctive molasses-like taste to the cookies. The ice cream should be made a day ahead; purchased low-fat frozen yogurt or sorbet can also be used.

COOKIES:

2½    cups whole-wheat flour
1½    teaspoons baking soda
1     teaspoon salt
½     cup (1 stick) unsalted butter, at room temperature
1     banana, puréed in a blender or food processor (½ cup purée)
¾     cup Sucanot (available at natural food stores)
¾     cup lightly packed light brown sugar
1     teaspoon vanilla extract
4     egg whites

8     ounces nondairy chocolate chips (available at natural food stores)
4     scoops Kathleen's Virtually No-Fat Chocolate Ice Cream (recipe follows)
4     ounces bittersweet chocolate, melted, or cocoa for dusting (optional)

KATHLEEN'S VIRTUALLY NO-FAT
CHOCOLATE ICE CREAM:

4     pounds slightly overripe bananas, peeled (10 to 15 bananas)
⅓     cup unsweetened cocoa

To make the cookies: Preheat the oven to 280°F. Line a baking sheet with parchment paper or aluminum foil. In a medium bowl stir the flour, baking soda, and salt together. Set aside. In another medium bowl beat the butter, banana purée, Sucanot, and brown sugar until fluffy. Beat in the vanilla, egg whites, and chips. Stir in one-fourth of the reserved dry ingredients, then fold in the remainder until blended. The batter will be thick and chunky. Scoop 2 tablespoons of batter for each cookie and drop 3 inches apart on the prepared baking sheet. Bake for 12 to 15 minutes until golden brown. Let cool before removing from the pan. The cookies will be chewy; if you prefer them crunchy, bake them at 320°F.

Place a cookie on each serving plate and top with a scoop of ice cream. Lean another cookie against the ice cream. Drizzle with melted chocolate or dust with cocoa if desired.

To make Kathleen's virtually no-fat chocolate ice cream: Line a baking sheet with parchment paper or waxed paper and place the bananas on the paper. Freeze overnight. Remove from the freezer and place in the bowl of a food processor. Add the cocoa. Pulse until smooth and creamy. If necessary, this can be done in two batches. Freeze in an ice cream freezer according to the manufacturer's instructions.

✍ *Variations:* Add 1 teaspoon flavored extract such as almond or peppermint; or 1 teaspoon liqueur such as Grand Marnier or crème de menthe; or the grated zest of $\frac{1}{2}$ orange and 1 cup almonds, crushed.

# Chocolate Ganache

*Robert Linxe*

LA MAISON DU CHOCOLAT
PARIS/NEW YORK

Robert Linxe has given four variations of his famous chocolate ganache.

**GANACHE WITH LEMON ZEST:**

| | |
|---|---|
| 2 | small lemons |
| 2 | cups heavy (whipping) cream |
| 4 | cups finely chopped chocolate |
| | Melted chocolate |

**GANACHE WITH MINT:**

| | |
|---|---|
| 2 | cups heavy (whipping) cream |
| ½ | cup fresh mint leaves |
| 4 | cups finely chopped chocolate |
| | Melted chocolate |

**GANACHE WITH RASPBERRIES:**

| | |
|---|---|
| ½ | cup fresh raspberries |
| 1 | tablespoon water |
| 1 | teaspoon sugar |
| 2 | cups heavy (whipping) cream |
| 4 | cups finely chopped chocolate |
| | Melted chocolate |

**GANACHE WITH GINGER:**

| | |
|---|---|
| 1 | fresh ginger root, peeled |
| 2 | cups heavy (whipping) cream |
| 4 | cups finely chopped chocolate |
| | Melted chocolate |

*To make the ganache with lemon zest:* Grate the zest of the lemons into the cream. In a saucepan bring the cream to a boil 3 times. Pour the cream over the chocolate. Stir slowly and gently from the center of the bowl. When the chocolate is melted and the cream is incorporated, pour the ganache onto a parchment-lined tray. Spread with a spatula to make a smooth 1-inch thick layer. Let cool 12 hours or overnight.

Heat a knife and cut the ganache into 1x1½-inch pieces. Coat the ganache with a thin layer of melted chocolate. Cool.

*To make the ganache with mint:* In a saucepan bring the cream to a boil 2 times. Return to a boil for the third time, and add the fresh mint leaves. Simmer gently for 1 minute to infuse the mint into the cream. Strain the cream directly over the chocolate. Stir slowly and gently from the center to combine. Whisk for 1 minute. When the chocolate is melted and the cream is incorporated, pour the ganache onto a parchment-lined tray. Spread with a spatula to make a smooth 1-inch thick layer. Let cool 12 hours or overnight.

Heat a knife and cut the ganache into 1x1½-inch pieces. Coat the ganache with a thin layer of melted chocolate. Cool.

*To make the ganache with raspberries:* In a saucepan boil the raspberries with the water and sugar until the raspberries are soft. In a blender or food processor purée the raspberries, and strain through a fine sieve.

In a saucepan bring the cream to a boil. Add the raspberry purée. Do not stir. Bring to a boil the second time. Pour the mixture over the chocolate. Stir slowly and gently from the center to combine. Whisk for 1 minute. When the chocolate is melted and the cream is incorporated, pour the ganache onto a parchment-lined tray. Spread with a spatula to make a smooth 1-inch thick layer. Let cool 12 hours or overnight. Heat a knife and cut the ganache into 1x1½-inch pieces. Coat the ganache with a thin layer of melted chocolate. Cool.

❧ *To make the ganache with ginger:* In a saucepan bring the cream to a boil 2 times. Grate about 1 teaspoon of ginger root into the cream. Bring to a boil for the third time. Strain the mixture directly over the chocolate, pressing the ginger solids against the strainer to release the flavor. Stir slowly and gently from the center to combine. Whisk for 1 minute. When the chocolate is melted and the cream is incorporated, pour the ganache onto a parchment-lined tray. Spread with a spatula to make a smooth 1-inch thick layer. Let cool 12 hours or overnight. Heat a knife and cut the ganache into 1x1½-inch pieces. Coat the ganache with a thin layer of melted chocolate. Cool.

# Chocolate Bag with White Chocolate Mousse

### Jackie Chen
JACKIE'S
CHICAGO, ILLINOIS

**SERVES 12**

MOUSSE:

| | |
|---|---|
| 12 | ounces white chocolate, chopped |
| 1 | envelope (¼ ounce) unflavored gelatin |
| 1 | cup milk |
| 1 | cup heavy (whipping) cream |
| 4 | egg whites |
| | Squeeze of lemon juice |

CHOCOLATE BAGS:

| | |
|---|---|
| 2½ | pounds semisweet chocolate, melted |

| | |
|---|---|
| 12 | waxed paper bags, approximately 3 inches wide and 8½ inches tall, with square bottoms (see Note below) |

RASPBERRY SAUCE:

| | |
|---|---|
| 16 | ounces frozen raspberries |

ASSEMBLY:

Fresh strawberries

✍ *To make the mousse:* In the top of a double boiler over barely simmering water melt the chocolate. In a small bowl dissolve the gelatin in ¼ cup of milk.

In a saucepan bring the remaining milk to a boil. In a bowl gradually combine the melted chocolate and hot milk. Add the dissolved gelatin and stir until the mixture is smooth and well blended. Cool the mixture over a bowl of ice water, stirring occasionally until partially set.

Beat the whipping cream until stiff and refrigerate. Beat the egg whites to soft peaks. Add the lemon juice and beat until stiff. Carefully fold together the whipped cream and egg whites. Gently add the chocolate mixture. Refrigerate the mousse overnight or up to 3 days.

✍ *To make the chocolate bags:* Trim the top of a bag by half, to 4 inches tall. Open the bag, making sure that the bottom and sides are straight. Fold the top edge of the bag over so that the bag sits squarely. With a brush, "paint" the inside of the bag with melted chocolate. Repeat with all of the bags. Freeze overnight (the bags will hold for 2 to 3 days in the freezer).

Note: 1-quart freezer bags can be adapted. Cut each bag to 5 inches tall and fold over the top 2 inches. Open the bag fully; tuck the bottom corners under to form a flat base. Secure with tape.

✍ *To make the raspberry sauce:* In a food processor purée raspberries. Strain and refrigerate.

✍ *To assemble:* Spoon chilled raspberry sauce onto serving plates. Just before serving, in a cool place, carefully peel the waxed bag off the set chocolate. Spoon the white chocolate mousse into the chocolate bag and top with stemmed, halved strawberries. If desired, garnish with whipped cream, sliced kiwi, and whole strawberries.

# White Chocolate

🌾

## Terrine of White Chocolate and Praline
## with Coconut Tile Cookies and Caramel Sauce

*Dennis Hutley*
THE VERSAILLES RESTAURANT
NEW ORLEANS, LOUISIANA

**SERVES 6**

Crisp, shaped tile cookies provide a contrast in texture to the pecan-studded white chocolate terrine.

### TERRINE OF WHITE CHOCOLATE AND PRALINE:

6    ounces white chocolate, chopped
¼    cup (½ stick) unsalted butter
2    teaspoons plain gelatin
¼    cup praline or other nut liqueur or brandy, chilled
¾    cup heavy (whipping) cream
½    cup chopped pecans, blanched almonds, or peeled hazelnuts (page 190)

### CARAMEL SAUCE:

¼    cup sugar

1    tablespoon unsalted butter
½    cup heavy (whipping) cream

### COCONUT TILE COOKIES:

*(Makes 6)*
1    egg
¼    cup shredded coconut
¼    cup sugar
1½   teaspoons all-purpose flour

½    cup heavy (whipping) cream
     *Fresh mint sprigs, candied flowers or fruit, and unsweetened cocoa for garnish*

---

🍃 *To make the terrine:* In a double boiler over barely simmering water melt the chocolate and butter, stirring until smooth. Sprinkle the gelatin over the liqueur in a small cup and set aside. In a small saucepan over medium heat bring ¼ cup of cream to a boil, and stir it gradually into the chocolate mixture. Add the gelatin-liqueur mixture, then the pecan pieces, and mix well. Refrigerate until chilled, stirring occasionally.

---

In a small, deep bowl beat the remaining ½ cup of cream until stiff peaks form. Fold into the chocolate mixture. Line a 4-cup mold with plastic wrap, pour in the terrine mixture, and chill for at least 2 to 3 hours.

    *To make the caramel sauce:* Place the sugar in a small skillet or saucepan over medium-low heat. When the sugar starts to turn color around the edges, begin to shake and swirl the pan to uniformly brown the sugar. When it becomes thoroughly golden brown, add the butter and mix well. Stir in the cream gradually, being very careful of the resulting steam from the saucepan. Remove from the heat, transfer to a clean container, and let cool.

    *To make the coconut tile cookies:* Preheat the oven to 375°F. Place a large baking sheet in the oven to preheat. In a small bowl beat the egg and stir in the coconut, sugar, and flour. Remove the baking sheet from the oven and coat well with shortening or spray with cooking oil. Stirring well each time, drop the batter 4 to 5 inches apart on the pan. Bake for about 10 minutes or until the outside edges are brown and the cookies are crisp-looking almost to the center. If the oven rack or baking sheet is not level, the wafers will run together. If this happens, about halfway through baking cut the cookies apart with the edge of a metal spatula. Leaving the pan in the oven with oven door open, remove one cookie with a metal spatula, transfer to a cool surface and roll into a cylinder; hold the shape in place 15 to 20 seconds, then set aside. Repeat until the remaining wafers are shaped. Keep in a cool, dry place.

    *To serve:* In a medium bowl whip ½ cup of heavy cream until stiff peaks form. Stand a cookie upright in the top center of each of 6 chilled plates. Unmold and unwrap the terrine and cut it into 12 even slices. Place 2 slices on the left side of each cookie and spoon about 2 tablespoons of caramel sauce onto the left side of each plate. Using a pastry bag fitted with a fluted top, pipe a mound of freshly whipped cream next to the cookie. Garnish with mint sprigs, candied violets or rose petals, or candied fruit, and dust the border of the plates with cocoa from a sugar shaker.

# White Chocolate Bread Pudding

*Dick Brennan, Jr.*
PALACE CAFE
NEW ORLEANS, LOUISIANA

### SERVES 8 TO 10

Chef Dick Brennan says that this is the most-requested recipe at Palace Café in New Orleans: a rich bread pudding flavored with white chocolate and topped with a warm white chocolate sauce.

BREAD PUDDING:

3    cups heavy (whipping) cream
10   ounces white chocolate, chopped
1    cup milk
½    cup sugar
2    eggs
8    egg yolks

1    loaf French bread, cut into ¼-inch thick slices
2    tablespoons chocolate shaving for garnish

WHITE CHOCOLATE SAUCE:

8    ounces white chocolate, chopped
⅓    cup heavy (whipping) cream

*To make the bread pudding:* Preheat the oven to 275°F. In a medium saucepan heat the cream but do not boil. Remove from the heat, add the white chocolate, and stir until melted and smooth. In a double boiler over barely simmering water beat the milk, sugar, eggs, and egg yolks together, and heat until warm. Blend the egg mixture into the cream and chocolate mixture.

Place the bread slices in a baking pan. Pour half of the chocolate mixture over the bread. Let sit for 30 minutes, then pour in the rest of the chocolate mixture. Cover with aluminum foil and bake for 15 minutes or until golden brown.

*To make the white chocolate sauce:* In a double boiler over barely simmering water melt the chocolate, stirring until smooth. Remove from the heat and mix in the heavy cream. Keep warm. To store, let cool slightly and store in an airtight jar in the refrigerator. Melt over barely simmering water and stir until smooth.

*To serve:* Spoon the pudding hot out of the pan, top with warm sauce, and garnish with chocolate shavings. Or, let cool to room temperature for about 45 minutes, loosen the sides, and invert the pan to unmold. Cut into squares. Top each serving with warm sauce and sprinkle with chocolate shavings.

# Swans with White Chocolate Mousse

Dominique Leborgne
LE PALAIS DU CHOCOLAT
WASHINGTON, D.C.

**SERVES 8**

These decorative cream puff swans are quite simple to make, and the white chocolate mousse filling is delicious. If making the swans is intimidating, simply form the cream puff dough into
round puffs or long éclairs.

CREAM PUFFS:

| | |
|---|---|
| ½ | cup water |
| ½ | cup milk |
| ½ | cup (1 stick) unsalted butter |
| ¾ | teaspoon sugar |
| ½ | cup plus 1 tablespoon all-purpose flour |
| 3 | eggs |

WHITE CHOCOLATE MOUSSE:

| | |
|---|---|
| 1½ | pounds white chocolate, chopped |
| 1 | envelope unflavored gelatin |
| 2 | tablespoons Amaretto liqueur |
| 4 | eggs |

| | |
|---|---|
| 4 | egg yolks |
| 3 | cups heavy (whipping) cream |

GARNISH:

| | |
|---|---|
| 6½ | ounces white chocolate, chilled |
| 1 | cup fresh or thawed frozen unsweetened rasp-berries |
| 1 | tablespoon sugar |
| 1 | tablespoon fresh lemon juice |
| | Confectioners' sugar for dusting |
| | Fresh raspberries |
| | Mint leaves |

➢ *To make the cream puffs:* Preheat the oven to 325°F. In a medium saucepan combine the
water, milk, butter, and sugar, and bring to a boil over medium-high heat. Remove the pan from
the heat and add the flour all at once. Stir quickly to combine and return the pan to the heat.
Cook, stirring constantly with a wooden spoon, until the mixture forms a ball and leaves a film
on the bottom of the pan. Scrape the mixture into a large bowl or a food processor and beat in 1
egg at a time.

Line a baking sheet with parchment paper or butter it. Spoon some of the dough into a pastry
bag fitted with a ½-inch star tip. Pipe the dough into 24 teardrop shapes 2 inches apart at one
end of the prepared pan to form the bodies of the swans. Place the remaining dough in a parchment cone with a snipped tip. To make the neck and head of the swans, pipe 30 long S shapes
with an oval at one end onto the other end of the pan; you will need extra necks/heads since
they are very fragile and some may break in assembling the swans. Bake the puffs in a preheated
oven for 20 minutes or until light brown. Set aside and let cool.

➢ *To make the mousse:* In a bowl over a pan of barely simmering water melt the white chocolate, stirring until smooth; set aside. Sprinkle the gelatin over the Amaretto in a cup. Place the

eggs and the egg yolks in a medium bowl then place the bowl over a pan of simmering water. Beat the eggs and egg yolks until they are warmed through. Remove the eggs from heat and add gelatin mixture, and whisk to combine. Whisk in the melted white chocolate, and set aside.

In a deep bowl whip the cream until stiff peaks form. Fold the whipped cream into the white chocolate mixture. Cover and chill the mousse until set.

*To assemble:* Cut each swan body in half crosswise and pull out any cooked dough, leaving only the crisp shell. Cut each top in half lengthwise to form the wings. Place the mousse in a pastry bag fitted with a fluted tip and pipe the mousse into the bottom part of the shell, forming the body of the swan. Use the base of mousse to anchor the head and neck piece of pastry. Add the wings, turning the browner portion to the inside. Pipe more mousse between the wings and over the base of the neck.

*To make the garnish:* Chop 2½ ounces of the white chocolate and melt it in a bowl over the pan of barely simmering water, stirring until smooth. Let cool slightly. Shave the remaining 4 ounces of white chocolate with a vegetable peeler to make about ¼ cup shavings. Combine the raspberries, sugar, and lemon juice in a blender or food processor and purée. Strain the raspberry purée through a fine-mesh sieve.

*To serve:* Fill the inside of each plate with the raspberry purée. Place the melted white chocolate in a parchment paper cone, snip the end, and pipe a design over the purée with the white chocolate. Place 2 or 3 swans on each plate, head to head. Top the mousse with white chocolate shavings to resemble feathers, then dust with confectioners' sugar. Arrange fresh raspberries and mint leaves around each swan and serve.

*Note:* The cream puffs, mousse, and raspberry sauce may be made up to 2 days in advance. Refrigerate the sauces, tightly covered. The swans must be assembled just prior to serving.

# White Chocolate–Mango Mousse

### Manuel Garcia

LA CASCATA, PRINCEVILLE HOTEL
PRINCEVILLE, KAUAI

**SERVES 8**

Fresh fruit and featherweight mousse create beautiful little cakes circled with a band of mango petals. The chocolate garnish can be used on almost any dessert; the dark and light contrasting bands of chocolate are particularly pretty against the golden mango.

CAKE:

| | |
|---|---|
| 1½ | cups (7 ounces) macadamia nuts, coarsely chopped |
| 1½ | cups confectioners' sugar |
| ⅔ | cup unsifted cake flour |
| 4 | whole eggs |
| 3 | egg whites |
| 3 | tablespoons sugar |
| 3 | tablespoons unsalted butter, melted |

MOUSSE:

| | |
|---|---|
| 2½ | ounces white chocolate, chopped |
| 1¼ | cups Mango Purée (page 187) |
| 2 | egg whites |
| 2½ | cups heavy (whipping) cream |
| 2 | egg yolks |
| ⅓ | cup sugar |

| | |
|---|---|
| 1 | envelope plain gelatin |
| ¼ | cup cold water |

GARNISH:

| | |
|---|---|
| 4 | mangos, peeled, cut from pit, and cut into thin slices |
| 1½ | tablespoons apricot jelly |
| 8 | fresh strawberries, hulled and cut into cross-wise slices |
| 24 | fresh blackberries |
| ¼ | cup ganache |

CHOCOLATE COILS:

(Makes 8)

| | |
|---|---|
| 2 | ounces white chocolate |
| 2 | ounces milk chocolate |
| 2 | ounces dark bittersweet chocolate |

❧ *To make the cake:* Preheat the oven to 375°F. Line a jelly roll pan with parchment paper or aluminum foil. In a blender or food processor grind the nuts and the confectioners' sugar to a fine powder. In a large bowl sift together the flour and ground nut mixture. Regrind and resift particles that do not go through the sifter. Add the whole eggs, beating until the batter is thoroughly blended. Set aside.

In a large bowl beat the egg whites until foamy. Gradually beat in the sugar until the meringue forms stiff peaks. Stir a large spoonful of batter into the meringue to lighten it, then fold the remaining meringue into the batter. Stir a large spoonful of batter into the melted butter, then pour the butter into the batter and blend. Spread the batter evenly in the prepared pan and bake for 10 minutes or until just set. Let cool.

❧ *To make the mousse:* In a double boiler over barely simmering water melt the white chocolate. Strain the chocolate through a fine-mesh sieve and return to the double boiler to keep warm. Put one half of the mango purée in a medium bowl and place the bowl in a larger bowl of ice water. In a deep bowl beat the cream until soft peaks form. Cover and refrigerate.

In a medium bowl over hot water beat the egg yolks and ⅓ cup of sugar until foamy. Transfer the egg mixture to the bowl of an electric mixer and set to beat at medium-high speed.

Sprinkle the gelatin over the cold water and let set for 3 minutes. Meanwhile, in a small saucepan over low heat warm the other half of the mango purée. Do not overheat; it should just be tepid. Stir in the gelatin mixture and whisk gently until completely dissolved. Stir in the melted chocolate until smooth. Pour into the cool mango purée and stir to blend the warm and cool mixtures; you want to cool the purée to add the remaining ingredients, but not so much that it sets up in the bowl.

When the mango mixture is cooled and starting to thicken, remove the egg mixture from the mixer; it should be pale yellow in color and thick enough that a slowly dissolving ribbon forms when some of it is dribbled on the surface. Stir a large spoonful of the mango mixture into the egg mixture, blending well. Pour the egg mixture into the mango mixture and whisk gently to blend. Stir a large spoonful of mixture into the whipped cream, then gently fold the whipped cream into the mixture. Chill in the refrigerator.

*To serve:* Using eight 4-inch ring molds, cut cake circles and leave them in the bottoms of the molds. Reserve 24 mango slices. Line the inside walls of the molds with a ring of overlapping mango slices, slipping the last slice under the first to complete the circle. Ladle the mousse into the mango-lined molds. Level off with the back of a knife.

In a small pan over medium heat, slightly warm the jelly and stir to blend. Remove the molds from the refrigerator and cover the top of each with the jelly glaze. Place the molds on a baking sheet and refrigerate until the glaze sets. Fan 3 of the reserved mango slices on each dessert plate. Add a ring of overlapping strawberry slices and 3 blackberries. To remove the molds, lift each mold from the baking sheet with a wide metal spatula. With a thin-bladed knife, cut around the mold between the mousse and the mold to loosen. Using your fingers, set the mold on an inverted glass or other flat-bottomed object that is slightly smaller than the ring mold and press the mold down gently. Carefully lift the entire mousse assembly and place it on the plate next to the mango slices. Place the ganache in a squeeze bottle or pastry bag fitted with a very small tip and pipe a spiral around one side of the dish. Garnish each mousse with a chocolate coil.

*To make the chocolate coils:* You will need a Styrofoam block about 15 inches square, push pins, and eight 9x2-inch heavy, flexible plastic strips. Pin one end of each strip to the Styrofoam. Separately melt each chocolate in a double boiler over barely simmering water. Put each chocolate in a squeeze bottle. Squeeze strips of the chocolates out slightly to a ⅛-inch thickness with a long thin spatula. When the chocolate has cooled slightly but is still pliable, twist the strips of plastic with the chocolate into a spiral shape and pin the other end of each strip to the Styrofoam to keep the coils in place. Keep in a cool place until set. When ready to use, unpin the strips and gently peel away the plastic, leaving the chocolate coils.

# White Chocolate Mousse Cake with Frangelico Cream and Hazelnut Praline Sauce

*Albert Leach*

L'AUBERGE PROVENÇAL
WHITE POST, VIRGINIA

**SERVES 6 TO 8**

CHOCOLATE LAYER CAKE:

| | |
|---|---|
| 2 | ounces semisweet chocolate |
| ¾ | cup cake flour |
| ¾ | teaspoon baking powder |
| ¼ | cup plus 1 tablespoon unsalted butter |
| ¼ | cup firmly packed dark brown sugar |
| ⅓ | cup sugar |
| 1 | egg |
| ⅓ | cup plus 1 tablespoon milk |

WHITE CHOCOLATE MOUSSE:

| | |
|---|---|
| 2½ | cups heavy (whipping) cream |
| 3 | teaspoons unflavored gelatin (1 pack) |
| 6 | tablespoons water |
| 8 | ounces white chocolate, chopped |
| 6 | tablespoons unsalted butter, at room temperature |
| 4 | eggs, separated |
| 4 | tablespoons sugar |

DARK CHOCOLATE GLAZE:

| | |
|---|---|
| 4 | ounces semisweet dark chocolate |
| 2 | tablespoons unsalted butter |
| 2 | tablespoons water |

FRANGELICO CREAM:

| | |
|---|---|
| 1 | cup milk |
| ⅓ | cup whipping cream |
| 5 | egg yolks |
| ⅔ | cup sugar |
| 2 | tablespoons Frangelico liqueur |

HAZELNUT PRALINE SAUCE:

| | |
|---|---|
| ½ | cup sugar |
| ⅓ | cup water |
| 1 | cup hazelnuts |

To make the chocolate layer cake: Preheat the oven to 350°F. Butter one 9-inch layer pan. Line the base of the pan with parchment paper. Butter the paper. Flour the pan and lined base. Tap to remove the excess flour.

In the top of a double boiler over low heat melt the chocolate, stirring occasionally. Stir until smooth. Cool to room temperature.

In a medium bowl sift together the flour and baking powder. In the bowl of an electric mixer combine the butter, brown sugar, and sugar, and beat on high speed until smooth and fluffy. Add the egg, mixing very thoroughly. Beat in the melted chocolate at medium speed. Using the lowest speed, blend in one-fourth of the flour mixture and one-third of the milk. Repeat with the remaining flour and milk in two additions. Continue beating until the batter is well mixed. Pour into the prepared pan and spread evenly. Bake for 25 minutes or until a cake tester inserted in the center comes out clean. Cool in the pan for 5 minutes. Invert onto a cake rack. Carefully remove the paper, and cool the cake completely.

*To make the white chocolate mousse:* Oil the inner side of a 9x3-inch springform pan. Put the cake layer in the springform pan. Chill a large mixing bowl and beater for the whipping cream. Refrigerate 2 cups of cream. In a small cup sprinkle the gelatin over the water, and let stand for 5 minutes while doing the chocolate mixture. In a double boiler or in a heatproof bowl over hot, not simmering, water combine the white chocolate and remaining $\frac{1}{2}$ cup of cream. Stir occasionally when partially melted. When melted, remove from the pan of water and whisk until smooth. Whisk in the butter.

Set the cup of gelatin in a shallow pan of hot water over low heat and melt, stirring often, for about 3 minutes. Stir into the chocolate mixture. Add the egg yolks one at a time, stirring vigorously after each addition.

In a dry bowl beat the egg whites using dry beaters at medium speed until soft peaks form. Gradually beat in the sugar and continue beating until the whites are stiff and shiny but not dry. Fold one-fourth of the whites into the chocolate mixture. Return the mixture to the egg whites and fold gently until blended. Whip the cream until nearly stiff. Fold the cream into the chocolate mixture, blending thoroughly. Pour the white chocolate mousse mixture into the prepared pan. Smooth the top and refrigerate for about 4 hours or until set.

*To make the dark chocolate glaze:* In the top of a double boiler over water that is at a low boil combine the dark chocolate, butter, and water. Let melt. Stir until smooth. Remove from the pan, and let cool to room temperature or until thickened.

Pour the dark chocolate glaze over the center of the chilled mousse and spread with a metal spatula.

Just before the chocolate hardens, precut slices just through the chocolate layer. Chill in the refrigerator.

*To make the Frangelico cream:* In a saucepan bring the milk and cream to a boil. Remove from the heat. In a mixing bowl beat the egg yolks and sugar together until pale. Add the heated milk and cream. Transfer the mixture back to the saucepan and return to medium heat, stirring constantly until the mixture thickens and coats the back of a spoon. Remove from the stove and put through a strainer or sieve. Let cool. Add the Frangelico liqueur.

*To make the hazelnut praline sauce:* In a saucepan bring the water and sugar to a boil. Keep boiling until it caramelizes to a medium brown. Add the hazelnuts, stirring quickly. Transfer onto waxed paper. Let cool. Break into smaller pieces and put into a food processor. Grind coarsely.

*To serve:* Release the chocolate mousse cake from the springform pan. Cut into slices. Spoon Frangelico Cream onto each serving plate. Place a slice of chocolate mousse cake over the sauce. Top with a sprinkling of coarsely ground hazelnut praline.

# White Chocolate Ravioli

*Jimmy Schmidt*
THE RATTLESNAKE CLUB
DETROIT, MICHIGAN

**SERVES 8**

## CHOCOLATE MOUSSE FILLING:

8    ounces extra-bittersweet chocolate or other high-quality dark chocolate, coarsely chopped

4    tablespoons unsalted butter

2    eggs, separated and at room temperature
     Pinch salt
     Pinch cream of tartar

¼    cup sugar

¼    cup heavy (whipping) cream, chilled

1    teaspoon vanilla extract

## HAZELNUT SAUCE:

¾    cup hazelnuts

1¼   cups half and half, scalded

5    egg yolks at room temperature

¼    cup sugar

¼    teaspoon vanilla extract
     Pinch salt

2    tablespoons Frangelico (hazelnut liqueur)

## RAVIOLI:

7    3-ounce bars imported white chocolate, preferably Tobler

## GARNISH:

½    cup chopped, toasted hazelnuts

8    mint sprigs

---

*To make the chocolate mousse filling:* In the top of a double boiler over barely simmering water melt the chocolate and butter. Stir until smooth, then transfer to a medium bowl. Whisk in the egg yolks quickly, one at a time. In a separate bowl beat the egg whites with the salt and cream of tartar at medium speed until frothy. Increase the speed to high and gradually add 2 tablespoons of the sugar, beating until the whites are stiff but not dry. Beat the cream with the remaining sugar and the vanilla until slightly thickened. Fold the egg whites and then the whipped cream into the chocolate and chill, covered with plastic wrap, overnight.

*To make the hazelnut sauce:* Toast the hazelnuts on a baking sheet in a 350°F oven for 10 minutes, or until browned. Place the nuts in the center of a tea towel, cover them with the towel, and let them steam for 2 minutes. Rub them with the towels to remove the skins. Place the nuts and hot half and half in a blender or a food processor fitted with a steel blade and blend until the nuts are coarsely chopped. Cool completely, or refrigerate overnight.

In a heavy saucepan or in the top of a double boiler combine the egg yolks, sugar, vanilla, and salt and whisk in the nut cream. Stir over low heat until the mixture heats and slightly thickens; foam will come to the top and it will barely coat the back of a spoon. Stir constantly while heating and do not allow it to come to a boil or the yolks will curdle. Remove from the heat and strain into a bowl. Stir into the Frangelico and refrigerate until needed.

♨ *To make the ravioli:* Chill a ravioli mold in the freezer. Preheat the oven to its lowest setting for 5 minutes and then turn it off. Break the chocolate bars in half lengthwise and place them on a baking sheet in the turned off oven for about 5 minutes, or until the chocolate is soft enough to be pliable and give to the pressure of a finger.

Roll 1 piece of chocolate out on a sheet of parchment paper to flatten it enough to fit through a pasta machine set on the widest setting. Run the chocolate through the pasta machine rollers, decreasing the setting each time until the chocolate sheet is $\frac{1}{16}$ inch thick.

Quickly press the chocolate into the chilled ravioli mold and fill each ravioli with 1 to $1\frac{1}{2}$ tablespoons of the mousse. Roll a second sheet in the same manner and press it on the top of the ravioli, sealing it with a rolling pin.

Invert the mold, pressing gently to release the ravioli, and cut them into separate pieces with a ravioli cutter or knife. Place on a chilled baking sheet in the refrigerator and repeat with more sheets of chocolate, softening them in a warm oven as necessary.

♨ *To serve:* Let the ravioli stand at room temperature for 30 minutes. Spoon $\frac{1}{4}$ cup of sauce on each plate, and place 4 ravioli on top. Sprinkle with nuts and garnish with mint.

♨ *Note:* While no one will deny that this dessert is a lot of work, none of it need be last minute. The filling and sauce can be made 2 days in advance and the completed ravioli can be refrigerated for 2 days, tightly wrapped, before serving.

# White Chocolate Black Jack Ice Cream Sandwiches

## Allen Rubin White

HERMITAGE HOTEL
NASHVILLE, TENNESSEE

**SERVES 4**

WHITE CHOCOLATE BLACK JACK
ICE CREAM:

½     cup heavy (whipping) cream
1     cup cold whole milk
½     vanilla bean, split lengthwise and scraped
5     egg yolks
½     cup sugar
5     ounces white chocolate
2     tablespoons Jack Daniel's whiskey

PECAN MERINGUES:

5     egg whites
      Pinch salt

1     cup sugar
½     cup finely chopped pecans

SAUCE:

1     cup white wine
2     cups water
2     vanilla beans
6     peaches
¼     cup honey
2     tablespoons fresh lemon juice

      Fresh blackberries for garnish

*To make the white chocolate black jack ice cream:* In a large saucepan combine the cream, milk, and vanilla bean, and bring just to a boil over medium-high heat. Remove the pan from the heat, cover, and let rest for 15 to 20 minutes. In the bowl of an electric mixer fitted with a balloon whisk, whisk the egg yolks with the sugar.

Remove the vanilla bean from the saucepan. In a steady stream gradually whisk about one-third of the cream into the egg mixture. Add this mixture to the remaining cream-milk mixture in the saucepan and cook over medium-low heat, stirring constantly with a wooden spoon for about 5 minutes or until the custard thickens enough to coat the back of a spoon (180°F on a candy thermometer). Do not let the custard boil. Strain the custard through a fine mesh strainer into a metal bowl set in an ice bath. Stir occasionally until cold.

In the top of a double boiler set over simmering water melt the white chocolate. Stir the chocolate into the cooled custard and strain once more. Stir in the whiskey, cover, and refrigerate until chilled. When well chilled, pour into the canister of an ice cream maker and freeze according to the manufacturer's directions. Remove the ice cream from the ice cream maker and spread in a shallow 10x12-inch pan to a thickness of about ½ inch. Freeze until firm. While the ice cream is freezing, prepare the meringues that will be used to make the sandwiches.

*To make the pecan meringues:* Preheat the oven to 250°F. Line a baking pan with parchment paper. Trace 4-inch circles onto the parchment paper. In the bowl of an electric mixer beat the egg whites and salt together until they just hold soft peaks. Add the sugar in a stream and beat until the meringue holds stiff, glossy peaks. Gently fold in the chopped pecans. Spoon the meringue mixture into a pastry bag and pipe spirals onto the drawn circles. Fill in the circles completely. Completed circles should be about ¼ inch thick. Smooth the tops with a rubber spatula or table knife. Place the meringues in the preheated oven and bake 1 hour and 30 minutes or until dry. Remove the paper with the meringues and cool on a wire rack. When cooled, lift the meringues from the paper. Set aside until ready to use.

*To make the ice cream sandwiches:* Remove the ice cream from the freezer, and using a cookie cutter, cut the ice cream into circles the same diameter as the meringues. Carefully lift the ice cream circles from the pan with a rubber spatula, and place on the smooth side of one of the meringue shells. Top with another shell. The sandwiches may be assembled and stored in the freezer while the sauce is prepared.

*To make the sauce:* In a heavy-bottomed saucepan bring the wine and water to a simmer. Split and scrape the vanilla beans into the simmering mixture. Add the peaches to the liquid and poach until the skin begins to pull away. With a slotted spoon remove the peaches from the pan, and place them in a bowl of ice water just long enough to stop the cooking process. Meanwhile, reduce the peach cooking liquid over high heat to 1 cup or until a syrupy consistency is achieved. Strain the liquid into a container to remove the vanilla seeds, and add the honey and lemon juice.

Remove the peaches from the ice water. Peel, slice in half, and remove the pit. Slice the peach halves into 4 sections and remove any remaining pit material with a small melon baller. Add the peaches to the bowl with the syrup, and let steep until the syrup has cooled.

*To serve:* Preheat the broiler. Dust an assembled ice cream sandwich with confectioners' sugar and lightly caramelize the top by placing under the broiler for 10 seconds. Place the sandwiches in the center of individual dessert plates and surround with the peach sauce. Garnish with fresh blackberries and finely chopped pecans.

# White Chocolate-Passion Fruit Mousse and Crisp Fettuccine Napoleon with Mango Ginger Sauce

*Hans Röckenwagner*
RÖCKENWAGNER
SANTA MONICA, CALIFORNIA

**SERVES 8**

MANGO GINGER SAUCE:

1   cup fresh orange juice
1   tablespoon minced fresh ginger
1   mango, peeled, flesh removed from the seed
      and cubed

FILO NAPOLEONS:

½   pound filo pastry, thawed

MOUSSE:

7   ounces Ghirardelli white chocolate, chopped
      into small pieces

4   egg yolks
2   tablespoons sugar
4   egg whites
2   cups heavy (whipping) cream
⅓   cup passion fruit purée (available at specialty
      markets)

FINISHING:

⅓   cup blackberries or blueberries
⅓   cup strawberries, hulled and halved
⅓   cup raspberries
4   oranges, peeled and separated into segments

❧ *For the mango ginger sauce:* In a small saucepan bring the orange juice and ginger to a boil. Simmer for 2 minutes. Add the cubed mango. Remove the pan from the heat and allow to cool.

In a blender or food processor purée the mixture until smooth. Push through a fine sieve and refrigerate.

❧ *For the filo napoleons:* Preheat the oven (convection if possible) to 400°F. If the filo is not already in a roll, roll it up. Cut across the roll in ½-inch intervals to form 8 spirals of filo, along with the paper that separates each sheet of pastry. Toss each portion of pastry strips with your fingers to loosen and separate them. Remove the strips of paper so that you have filo "fettuccine."

On a baking sheet gently mound the fettuccine into 16 circles 3 inches in diameter. Bake for 5 to 7 minutes or until crisp but not at all brown. Cool on a rack and set aside.

❧ *For the mousse:* In the top of a double boiler over barely simmering water melt the chocolate. Set aside.

In a large bowl combine the egg yolks with 1 tablespoon of the sugar and whisk over the simmering water until pale and thickened. In a separate bowl whisk the egg whites to soft peaks. Add the remaining tablespoon of sugar and whisk until glossy but not dry. In a third bowl whisk the cream and passion fruit purée together to soft peaks.

Fold the egg yolk mixture gently into the melted chocolate. Then fold in the egg whites, and finally the whipped cream mixture, being careful not to crush too much air out of the mousse. Transfer to a stainless steel bowl and refrigerate for at least 2 hours.

*To assemble:* Using eight 4-inch wooden skewers, skewer the berries alternately to form a fruit "kabob." On each of 8 serving plates make a pool of mango sauce and fan out 5 or 6 orange segments in the sauce. Place a filo circle in the center. Using a tablespoon dipped in very hot water, shape quenelles out of the white chocolate mousse and place 2 of them over each napoleon. Top with a second filo circle. Spear a skewer through the center of each napoleon and serve immediately.

# Napoleon of Tropical Fruit

*Patrice Serenne*
MARK'S PLACE
MIAMI, FLORIDA

**SERVES 8**

This tropical interpretation of the napoleon consists of passion fruit and key lime curds, white chocolate mousse, and phyllo dough triangles, served with a sauce of passion fruit seeds and raspberries. Both the curds and the mousse must be made the day before assembling and serving the dessert.

PASSION FRUIT CURD:

| | |
|---|---|
| 10 | to 12 passion fruits |
| ¾ | cup sugar |
| 5 | eggs |
| 4 | egg yolks |
| ½ | cup (1 stick) unsalted butter, cut into small pieces |
| 4 | ounces white chocolate, chopped |

KEY LIME CURD:

| | |
|---|---|
| ¾ | cup key lime juice |
| ¾ | cup sugar |
| 5 | eggs |
| 4 | egg yolks |
| ½ | cup (1 stick) unsalted butter, cut into small pieces |
| 4 | ounces white chocolate, chopped |

WHITE CHOCOLATE MOUSSE:

| | |
|---|---|
| ½ | cup light corn syrup |
| 13 | ounces white chocolate, chopped |
| ⅞ | cup sweetened condensed milk |

| | |
|---|---|
| ½ | cup light rum |
| 1 | envelope plain gelatin |
| 3 | cups heavy (whipping) cream |

PASTRY TRIANGLES:

| | |
|---|---|
| 6 | sheets phyllo dough |
| 2 | cups (4 sticks) unsalted butter, melted |
| 1 | cup sugar |

PASSION FRUIT–RASPBERRY SAUCE:

| | |
|---|---|
| 1 | cup reserved passion fruit seeds from Passion Fruit Curd |
| 1 | vanilla bean, halved lengthwise |
| 1 | cup Raspberry Sauce (page 187) |

GARNISH:

| | |
|---|---|
| 1 | large block white chocolate, at room temperature |
| | Sifted confectioners' sugar for dusting |
| 1 | fresh mango, peeled and diced |
| 8 | fresh mint sprigs |

🐾 *To make the passion fruit curd:* Squeeze the passion fruits to make ¾ cup of juice. Reserve the seeds. In a double boiler over simmering water whisk the juice, sugar, eggs, and egg yolks until the mixture becomes very thick, 5 to 10 minutes. Remove from the heat and stir in the butter, then the white chocolate. Cover and refrigerate the mixture overnight.

&#x1F34B; *To make the key lime curd:* Make the key lime curd in the same manner as the passion fruit curd, substituting the lime juice for the passion fruit juice. Cover and refrigerate overnight.

&#x1F34B; *To make the white chocolate mousse:* In a medium, heavy saucepan bring the corn syrup to a boil over medium heat. Remove the pan from the heat and add the chocolate. Whisk until the chocolate is melted, then add the milk and continue whisking until the mixture is blended. Set aside. In a small saucepan stir the rum and gelatin over low heat until the gelatin is completely dissolved. Stir the gelatin mixture into the chocolate mixture. Add the heavy cream and whisk all together. Strain the mixture into a bowl, cover, and refrigerate overnight. The next day, place the mousse in the bowl of an electric mixer and beat for 2 to 3 minutes until the mixture is light and fluffy. Take care not to overmix.

&#x1F34B; *To make the pastry triangles:* Preheat the oven to 375°F. Line a baking sheet with parchment paper or aluminum foil. Place 1 sheet of phyllo dough on a large cutting board. Keep the remaining dough covered with a towel to keep it moist. Lightly brush the phyllo with melted butter and sprinkle with some of the sugar. Repeat to make 6 layers of the phyllo. Cut the dough in half lengthwise, then divide each half into 8 equal squares. Cut each square in half diagonally, making 32 triangles. Transfer the triangles to the prepared pan. Cover the pastry with another sheet of parchment or foil and set a second pan on top. (The additional pan helps the triangles keep their shape and helps to caramelize the phyllo dough.) Bake the triangles for 8 to 10 minutes or until golden brown. The pastry burns easily, so watch carefully. Remove the top pan and paper or foil and let the pastries cool completely.

&#x1F34B; *To make the passion fruit–raspberry sauce:* In a small saucepan combine the passion fruit seeds and vanilla bean and cook over low heat for 8 to 10 minutes. Add the raspberry sauce and let cool. Remove the vanilla bean.

&#x1F34B; *To make the chocolate curls:* Place the white chocolate on a piece of parchment paper or waxed paper. Using a small ring mold or cookie cutter, pull the mold or cutter across the chocolate, making curls. Set aside in a cool place.

&#x1F34B; *To serve:* Place the passion fruit curd, key lime curd, and mousse in 3 separate pastry bags fitted with fluted tips. Place 1 pastry triangle on a large dessert plate with the wide end toward the center. Pipe a rosette of passion fruit curd on the wide end. Place another triangle on top at an angle from the first, so the points are fanned. Press down lightly to secure the triangle, and pipe a rosette of white chocolate mousse on the end of this triangle. Add a third triangle again at an angle, and pipe a rosette of key lime curd on it. Repeat with the remaining plates.

Dust the 8 remaining triangles with confectioners' sugar and place one on top of each dessert. Garnish the plates with the diced mango. Spoon the sauce around the plates and garnish with a mint sprig and 4 chocolate curls.

# White Chocolate Mousse in an Almond Cookie Shell

### *Masataka Kobayashi*
MASA'S, VINTAGE COURT HOTEL
SAN FRANCISCO, CALIFORNIA

**SERVES 6**

ALMOND COOKIE SHELL:

| | |
|---|---|
| 3 | *egg whites* |
| 2 | *tablespoons sugar* |
| 2 | *tablespoons all-purpose flour* |
| ½ | *cup almonds, sliced and toasted* |

MOUSSE:

| | |
|---|---|
| 1 | *cup sugar* |
| ½ | *cup water* |

| | |
|---|---|
| 8 | *egg whites* |
| 6 | *egg yolks* |
| 1 | *tablespoon white rum* |
| 1 | *pound white chocolate, melted* |
| | *Crème Fraîche (page 189)* |
| | *Raspberry Purée (page 187)* |

🍃 *To make the almond cookie shells:* Preheat the oven to 350°F. In a large bowl beat the egg whites briefly. Add the sugar and flour, then whisk. Stir the almonds into the mixture. Butter a sheet pan and spoon tablespoons of mixture onto the pan. Spread slightly with the back of a spoon to form circles about 2 inches apart. Bake for 5 to 7 minutes. Remove from the oven and while still hot mold into small cups by placing over a rolling pin. Set aside to dry.

🍃 *To make the mousse:* In a saucepan heat the sugar and water until it reaches the soft ball stage. In the bowl of a mixer beat the egg whites until medium stiff, beating first on medium then on high. Add the sugar and water to the egg whites and continue to beat briefly until a stiff meringue is formed. Place the egg yolks in a metal bowl and beat over simmering water with a whisk. Add the rum to the egg yolks, still beating over the heat. Fold the egg yolks into the egg whites. Fold the melted chocolate into the egg mixture. Refrigerate for 3 to 4 hours.

Serve one scoop of mousse in an almond cookie shell. Garnish with crème fraîche and raspberry purée.

# Garnishes, Sauces, and Accompaniments

## Chocolate Garnishes

Chocolate can be very tricky, "seizing" (stiffening) instantly if a drop of water accidently falls into the pan, "breaking" (separating) if heat is applied incorrectly, and requiring a "tempering" process for coating and molding work. Yet sculpted flowers, leaves, geometric pieces and filigree designs are worth the effort of learning to work with the temperamental ingredient.

The following recipe gives steps for forming garnishes used with desserts in this book, and the quantity will make at least enough of any one type to garnish four dessert plates. At any time while you are working chocolate, you can warm it just slightly with a heat lamp or blow dryer to keep it flexible. Any excess chocolate at any step can be scraped back into the pan and allowed to remelt. Chocolate garnishes can be held in the refrigerator or freezer until ready to use.

Hawaiian Vintage Chocolate is the only chocolate grown in the United States. Hawaiian chefs frequently use beautiful chocolate garnishes to complete masterpiece desserts.

*To make chocolate curls:* Melt 2 ounces chopped bittersweet chocolate in a double boiler and heat to 100°F. Let cool to 90°F. Pour the chocolate out on a baking sheet and spread it into a smooth layer ⅛ inch thick. When cool, scrape up narrow strips of chocolate with the back of your nail or a narrow spatula, creating small curls.

*To make flat chocolate shapes:* Place a heavy flexible plastic sheet on a work surface. Melt chopped bittersweet chocolate in a double boiler and heat to 100°F. Let cool to 90°F. Pour the chocolate out on the plastic and spread it out into a smooth layer of the desired thickness, usually just over ⅛ inch thick. Let cool to room temperature and use molds, cookie cutters, or the tip of a sharp knife to cut out the desired shapes. Pull the excess chocolate from around the shapes and place the designs in the refrigerator to set.

# Striped Chocolate

This recipe makes dark chocolate striped with white chocolate. To create dark lines on a white background, simply use the dark chocolate first. Striped chocolate is used in The Unforgettable Torte on page 26 and the Chocolate Macadamia Nut-Toffee Torte on page 64.

| | | | |
|---|---|---|---|
| 4 | ounces white chocolate, chopped | 8 | ounces bittersweet chocolate, chopped |

*❧* You will need a sheet of heavy, flexible plastic, a long, thin spatula, and a masonry comb. Melt chopped white chocolate in a double boiler and heat to 100°F. Let cool to 90°F. Pour the white chocolate out onto the plastic. With the spatula, spread the chocolate out to a thin layer of less than $\frac{1}{8}$ inch. Using the masonry comb, scrape through the chocolate down to the plastic to create straight lines in the chocolate. Refrigerate for about 5 minutes or until set.

Melt the chopped bittersweet chocolate in a double boiler and heat to 100°F. Let cool to 90°F. Remove the white chocolate lines from the refrigerator. With a clean spatula, spread the dark chocolate over the back of the stripes. Be careful not to disturb the stripes. Refrigerate for 5 minutes.

*❧ To make striped chocolate wings:* After the chocolate has set slightly, cut through the chocolate and plastic in the shape of wings with a sharp knife. Drape them across a curved surface, plastic side down. Refrigerate until set. At the same time, melt 4 ounces of bittersewet chocolate and spread it out just over 1/8-inch thick. Let cool, then cut into eight 4-inch plain chocolate disks; these become the bases to hold the chocolate wings. When set and ready to use, peel away the plastic to expose the shiny striped surface of the wings. Makes 8 wings.

*❧ To make striped chocolate tulip petals:* Let the chocolate set at room temperature and use a cookie cutter to stamp out the desired shapes. Pull the excess chocolate from around the cut shapes. Put the shapes, still on the plastic, in the refrigerator to firm completely. Peel the plastic from the designs. Makes 24 chocolate tulip petals.

*❧ Variation:* An alternate method of making striped chocolate is to pour and smooth a thin layer of chocolate, then pipe stripes of the same color or contrasting color chocolate on top of the smooth layer.

# Chocolate Ganache

12    *ounces semisweet chocolate, chopped*          1    *cup heavy (whipping) cream*

☙ In a double boiler over simmering water melt the chocolate. In a small saucepan bring the cream to a boil over medium heat. Stir the warm cream into the chocolate, being careful not to beat air into the mixture.

# Pulled Sugar

Pulled sugar is definitely in the "advanced" category of confectionery. Yet it makes spectacular garnishes, and, once pulled and worked into a shiny mass, it can be kept for months if you place it on a piece of clean limestone in an airtight container. Keep it workable by placing it under a heat lamp until warm, soft, and pliable.

4    *pounds sugar*                                     1    *teaspoon cream of tartar*
2    *cups water*                                             *Food coloring if desired*

☙ In a heavy, medium saucepan combine the sugar, water, and cream of tartar, and bring to a boil over medium heat. Cook until the syrup reaches 160°F. Do not stir the syrup during this time. When the temperature has reached 160°F, remove the pan from heat and set it in a pan of ice water to stop the cooking. The syrup will still be colorless.

When the syrup has cooled slightly, pour it out onto a marble slab or a baking sheet. Let it continue to cool. If desired, drop 4 or 5 large drops of food coloring randomly over the surface of the syrup as it cools. Brown coloring will result in a golden coloring; all colors will lighten considerably as the sugar is worked. When it appears to have thickened, put on heavy rubber gloves and lift the edges of the syrup; the syrup will pull away from the slab and fold back on itself. Use the palm of your hand to roll the edges in over the remainder of the syrup. Continue to lift the syrup over itself again and again, working slowly at first, then faster as the sugar cools. As it becomes cool enough to pull, it will hold its shape. When it is cool enough to handle, grasp the lump with both hands, lift it and quickly pull your hands apart, stretching the sugar. Let the center of the strip rest on the work surface and fold the ends across, folding the sugar strip in thirds. Lift again with both hands and twist as if you are wringing it. Repeat the pulling, folding, and twisting motions about 45 times, or until the sugar develops a deep shine (overpulling the sugar will kill the shine). It will look like mother of pearl. The wringing action helps distribute the color evenly throughout the mass; if you prefer the effect of fine straight lines of color, do not wring between folding. Place the sugar mass under a heat lamp to keep it pliable.

✒ *To make leaves or petals:* Using scissors, cut off a small piece of the sugar and press it into a leaf mold or other form. If creating flowers, press several of these "petals" together to form the flower.

✒ *To make spirals:* Working under the heat lamp, pull a piece of sugar from the lump and press it against a wooden dowel or spoon handle. Holding the sugar in place with your thumb, twist the dowel, pulling it away from the sugar to draw a thin twisting strand from the mass, until the desired length is reached. Pinch off the end from the lump, remove from the lamp area to cool, and slide the finished spiral off the dowel.

✒ *To make ribbons:* Working under a heat lamp, grasp a piece of sugar and pull a long, thin strip from the lump. Pinch or cut it off, stretch it as thin as desired, and twist and ruffle as desired. Remove from the lamp area and let cool.

# Simple Syrup

### MAKES 3 CUPS

| | | | |
|---|---|---|---|
| 2 | *cups water* | 1 | *cup sugar* |

✒ In a heavy, medium saucepan combine the sugar and water, and cook over high heat until the sugar dissolves and the mixtures reaches a full boil, about 3 minutes. Remove from the heat, let cool, and store in a covered container in the refrigerator for up to 3 weeks.

# Chocolate Sauce

### MAKES 4 CUPS

| | | | |
|---|---|---|---|
| 1 | *cup sugar* | 8 | *ounces bittersweet chocolate, chopped* |
| 2 | *cups half and half* | 8 | *ounces unsweetened chocolate, chopped* |

✒ In a large, heavy saucepan heat the sugar and half-and-half over medium-low heat until hot but not boiling. Add the chocolate and stir until the chocolate is melted and the mixture is smooth. Serve warm, or pour into a jar, cover, and refrigerate for up to 1 week.

# Uncooked Fruit Purée (Coulis)

**MAKES 2 CUPS**

| | | | |
|---|---|---|---|
| 4 | cups fresh berries, or 1 pound fresh fruit, peeled and cut into ½-inch dice | 2 | tablespoons sugar or more to taste |
| | | 1 | teaspoon fresh lemon juice (optional) |

In a food processor or blender purée the fruit until smooth. Strain the purée through a fine-mesh sieve. Stir in the sugar and lemon juice, adjusting to taste. Cover and refrigerate until needed. This purée may be used as an ingredient in another recipe or by itself.

*Lilikoi (passion fruit):* To use, cut the fruit in half and peel. For juice, press through a sieve and discard the pulp.

*Mango:* Lay the mango on its flattest side on a cutting board. With a small sharp knife, cut a thick slice off the top, avoiding the stone. Flip the fruit over and repeat the process on the other side. Cut away any flesh still clinging to the stone and discard the pit. Score the flesh inside the large halves, and, using your fingers, bend the skin backward until it is almost inside out, which spreads the chunks apart. Cut them away from the skin and proceed to purée or use as desired.

# Blackberry Sauce

**MAKES 2 CUPS**

| | | | |
|---|---|---|---|
| | Zest and juice of ½ orange | ¼ | cup sugar |
| | Zest and juice of ½ lemon | 1½ | cups fresh blackberries |
| 3 | tablespoons raspberry liqueur | 1 | vanilla bean, halved lengthwise |
| 3 | tablespoons crème de cassis | | |
| 1 | tablespoon Pernod or other anise-flavored liqueur | | |

In a saucepan combine all of the ingredients except ½ cup of the blackberries and the vanilla bean and heat over medium heat. Scrape the seeds from the vanilla bean and add the seeds and the pod to the pan. Bring to a boil. Cool for 3 minutes. Strain through a fine-mesh sieve. Add the remaining whole blackberries.

# Caramel Sauce

### MAKES 2 CUPS

This is a basic caramel sauce with a thick consistency enriched by both butter and cream.

| | | | |
|---|---|---|---|
| 1½ | cups sugar | 1 | cup heavy (whipping) cream, heated |
| ½ | cup water | ½ | teaspoon vanilla extract |
| 3 | tablespoons butter | | |

In a medium, heavy saucepan combine the sugar and water. Bring to a simmer over medium heat, swirling occasionally. Cover the pan, raise the heat to medium high, and cook for 2 minutes, or until the liquid gives off large, thick bubbles. Remove the cover and cook, swirling the syrup, until it turns golden brown.

Remove the pan from the heat and stir in the butter with a wooden spoon. Add the cream, stirring constantly, then add the vanilla. Return the pan to a low flame and stir constantly until any lumps have melted and the syrup is smooth. Serve warm over ice cream or cake, or pour into a jar, cover, and refrigerate for up to 1 week.

*Note:* To make butterscotch, substitute light brown sugar for the sugar and add 2 teaspoons of cider vinegar to the syrup along with the vanilla.

# Orange Zest Powder

| | | | |
|---|---|---|---|
| 2 | oranges | 1½ | cups water |
| 1 | cup sugar | | |

Preheat the oven to 275°F. Line a baking sheet with parchment paper or aluminum foil. Using a small knife or zester, remove the zest (outer colored skin) of the oranges without picking up any of the bitter white pith underneath. If you have used a knife, cut the zest into fine julienne.

In a small, heavy, nonaluminum saucepan cook the sugar and water together over medium-high heat for 2 minutes until the sugar is dissolved. Add the orange zest and cook for 10 minutes. With a slotted spoon, remove the zest from the syrup and place it in a single layer in the prepared pan. Bake about 20 minutes until the zest is very crisp. Let the zest cool, and grind it in a food processor or spice grinder to a very fine powder. Set aside.

# Crème Anglaise

**MAKES 2 CUPS**

| | | | |
|---|---|---|---|
| 4 | egg yolks | 2 | teaspoons vanilla extract |
| ⅓ | cup sugar | 1 | tablespoon butter, at room temperature |
| 1½ | cups milk | | (optional) |

&#10086; In a medium, heavy saucepan whisk the egg yolks over low heat until they are pale in color. Add the sugar 1 tablespoon at a time, beating well after each addition. Beat until the mixture reaches the consistency of cake batter.

Whisk in the milk, then stir constantly with a wooden spoon until the custard coats the spoon and a line drawn down the back of the spoon remains visible. Remove from heat and stir in the vanilla.

If the custard is to be chilled, press a sheet of plastic wrap directly onto the surface to prevent a skin from forming, or dot the top with bits of the optional butter. Chill the custard for up to 2 days.

&#10086; *Note:* If the custard begins to overheat and the egg yolks are forming lumps, remove it immediately from the heat and whisk briskly to cool the mixture. Push the custard through a fine-mesh sieve with the back of a spoon to remove the lumps. If it has not sufficiently thickened, return it to heat to complete cooking.

# Crème Fraîche

Crème fraîche is now widely available in specialty foods stores; however, it is also easy to make by combining 1 cup of heavy (whipping) cream (preferably not ultra-pasteurized) with 1 tablespoon of buttermilk in a small saucepan. Slowly heat the cream to warm, 105°F to 115°F. Pour the mixture into a clean glass container and cover it loosely. Set in a warm place (70°F to 80°F) until thickened, about 24 to 36 hours. Cover tightly and refrigerate for 1 more day to develop the tangy flavor.

# Toasting Nuts

Place shelled nuts in a large, dry skillet over low to medium heat. Cook, stirring and turning constantly with a spoon or spatula, until the nuts are heated through and just beginning to change color; do not let them turn brown. Remove the pan from the heat immediately and spread the nuts on a large plate or tray lined with paper towels to cool.

    Or spread the nuts in a single layer in a shallow pan. Bake in a preheated 350°F oven, shaking the sheet occasionally, for 5 to 12 minutes until the nuts or seeds are golden, depending on size. Let cool.

# Toasting and Peeling Hazelnuts

Toast hazelnuts in the oven as described above for 7 or 8 minutes or until the papery skin begins to flake. Roll the hazelnuts in a clean dish towel and let cool for several minutes. Rub the hazelnuts vigorously inside the towel until part of the skins have rubbed off. Pour them into a colander and stir them over the sink to release more of the skins.

# Shelling Macadamia Nuts

Macadamia nuts are round and extremely hard, making them very difficult to crack. They are readily available already shelled, but if you wish to do the job yourself, preheat the oven to 150°F. Spread the nuts in a single layer on a baking sheet and roast for 2 hours (very large nuts may roast for up to 4 hours). Let cool. Place a nut in the indent of a chopping block (or even a crack in the sidewalk) and rap it sharply with a hammer. The nuts will almost always come out whole. Macadamia nuts in the shell can be husked and kept in a basket in a dry place up to 6 months. Unshelled macadamias may be frozen and used as needed. To salt them, sauté the nuts in a little butter or oil. Lightly salt them, then cool and place in an airtight jar. Or, soak the nuts in salted water overnight, then place in a single layer on a baking sheet and dry for 1 hour at 150°F.

# Glossary

## ALMOND PASTE

A thick paste made of finely ground almonds, sugar, and water. Almond paste can be formed into sheets or molded into shapes. It is similar to marzipan, but marzipan is made from almond paste, confectioners' sugar, flavoring, and sometimes egg whites.

## CHOCOLATE

*Unsweetened:* Also referred to as baking or bitter chocolate, this is the purest of all cooking chocolates. A hardened chocolate liquor (which is the essence of the cocoa bean, not an alcohol), it contains no sugar and is usually packaged in a bar of eight blocks weighing 1 ounce each. Unsweetened chocolate must contain 50 to 58 percent cocoa butter.

*Bittersweet:* This chocolate is slightly sweetened with sugar, in amounts that vary depending on the manufacturer. It must contain 35 percent chocolate liquor and is used whenever an intense chocolate taste is desired. Bittersweet chocolate may be used interchangeably with semisweet chocolate in cooking and baking.

*Semisweet:* Sweetened with sugar, semisweet chocolate, unlike bittersweet, may have flavorings such as vanilla added to it. It is available in bar form as well as in chips and pieces.

*Milk:* A mild-flavored chocolate used primarily for candy bars but rarely (except for milk chocolate chips) in cooking. It may have as little as 10 percent chocolate liquor, but must contain 12 percent milk solids.

*Unsweetened cocoa powder:* Powdered chocolate that has had a portion of the cocoa butter removed.

*Dutch process cocoa powder:* Cocoa powder that has been treated to reduce its aciditiy. It has a more mellow flavor than regular cocoa, but it burns at a lower temperature.

*White chocolate:* Ivory in color, white chocolate is technically not chocolate at all: It is made from cocoa butter, sugar, and flavoring. It is difficult to work with, and should be used only in recipes that are specifically designed for it.

## CRÈME FRAÎCHE

While its tangy, tart flavor is similar to that of sour cream, crème fraîche is thinner and is used in cooking because it does not curdle when heated as do sour cream and yogurt.

## EDIBLE FLOWERS

Flowers add a beautiful tooch to dishes, and many flowers are edible. Make sure they are free of pesticides—your own garden is your surest supplier. Among edible blossoms are pansies, violas, and violets; roses, apple, peach, and plum blooms; geraniums; orange and lemon blossoms; nasturtiums; lavender;

jasmine; daisies; daylilies; dianthus; marigolds; and squash blooms.

## GANACHE

A filling or coating made from heavy cream and chocolate. It is also used to make chocolate truffles.

## GINGER

Fresh ginger is a brown, fibrous, knobby rhizome. It keeps for long periods of time. To use, peel the brown outside skin and slice, chop, or purée. It will keep indefinitely placed in a jar with sherry and refrigerated.

## GUAVA

A round tropical fruit with a yellow skin and pink inner flesh and many seeds. Grown commercially in Hawaii. The purée or juice is available as a frozen concentrate. Guava can also be made into jams, jellies, and sauces.

## KIWI

Kiwis hide their sweet green flesh in a fuzzy brown skin. Select fruit with few imperfections in the skin, and no very soft bruised spots. Peel the kiwi and slice; the seeds are edible.

## LILIKOI

The Hawaiian name for passion fruit, which is a small yellow, purple, or brown oval fruit of the passion fruit vine. The "passion" in passion fruit comes from the fact that its flower resembles a Maltese cross and refers to Christ's crucifixion, not to aphrodesiac qualities. The flavor is delicate but somewhat sharp, and perfumelike. Passion fruit is a natural substitute for lemon juice. Passion fruit concentrate can be found in the frozen juice section of many markets. Substitute oranges.

## MACADAMIA NUTS

A rich, oily nut grown mostly on the Big Island of Hawaii. Native to Australia. They're good, but expensive, canned.

## MANGO

A tropical fruit available in many supermarkets. A ripe mango has a smooth yellow to red skin and smells sweet; the yellow flesh is both sweet and tart. The skin should be peeled and the flesh cut away from the pit in strips. Papaya or fresh peaches can be substituted in many recipes. Mango purée is available frozen from confectioners' supply stores.

## MAPLE SYRUP

A sweet syrup made from the sugar-maple tree. Although it is expensive, do not substitute sugar syrup or a maple-syrup blend for pure maple syrup or the flavor will be inferior.

## MARZIPAN

A confection made from almond paste, confectioners' sugar, flavoring, and sometimes egg white. Marzipan is often used for shaped candies, such as fruit or flowers, or as a coating for cakes.

## MASCARPONE

A soft, fresh Italian cheese with a high fat content used primarily in desserts and for cheese tortas. If it is not available, combining equal parts of cream cheese and unsalted butter will produce a similar product.

## MERINGUE

Egg whites beaten until they are stiff but still glossy are called meringue, but the term also applies to dishes that are then sweetened and baked, such as meringue cookies and meringue toppings on pies.

## PAPAYA

The most common papaya used in Hawaii is the solo papaya, a tropical fruit with a yellow flesh, black seeds, and a perfumey scent. Other types are larger, and may have pink flesh; all are suitable for recipes. Papayas have a musky flavor with a slight citrus tang and are used primarily for desserts. They must be ripe when used or they will be bitter and acid.

## PARCHMENT PAPER

A white heat-resistant paper sold in rolls at cookware stores. It is used in cooking to line baking pans and baking sheets, to cook foods en papillote, and to loosely cover delicate foods like fish fillets during poaching.

## PASSION FRUIT

See lilikoi.

## PASTE FOOD COLORING

Available from confectioners' supply stores, paste food colors are more intense than the liquid food colors commonly found in supermarkets, and can be used like paints to obtain bright colors.

## PASTRY BAG

A bag, usually made of plastic, canvas, or nylon, that may be fitted with plain or decorative tips and used to pipe out icings, thick doughs, and puréed foods.

## PHYLLO (FILO) DOUGH

This tissue-paper thin pastry is made from a flour and water dough. Phyllo sheets are used in layers and brushed with butter or oil before baking. They are widely available in packages in the frozen section of supermarkets.

## PISTACHIO PASTE

A paste of ground pistachios available from confectioners' supply stores.

## POHA

The Hawaiian name for cape gooseberries, marble-sized tart berries encased in a papery husk.

## PRALINE PASTE

A paste made by cooking brown sugar until it has caramelized and thickened; chopped nuts are added. It is available from confectioners' supply stores.

## PRUNE PURÉE

A thick purée made from cut-up prunes moistened with water or other liquid. It is available in cans from confectioners' supply stores and some specialty foods stores.

## PUFF PASTRY

Flaky pastry that rises up to ten times its original height when baked. It is made from flour, water, butter, and salt. The distinctive flakiness results from adding the butter during a series of at least six rollings, turnings, and foldings that trap layers of butter and air between the layers of pastry. When baked, the butter melts and the air expands as steam, puffing up the pastry. It can be prepared at home, or purchased frozen.

## RAMEKIN

A ceramic ovenproof dish ranging in size from 4 to 8 ounces. They are used for baking custards and individual servings of many foods.

## SOUFFLÉ

While the word *soufflé* literally means "puffed," it refers to a hot or cold dish with a light texture that uses beaten egg whites to achieve height.

## VANILLA BEANS

The pods of a relative of the orchid, vanilla beans are green and have no flavor when picked; they are then cured by a process of sweating and drying. Once cured, the long, wrinkled black beans are either bundled whole for export or processed into extract.

## WATER BATH

A vessel of simmering water into which a cooking vessel is set in order to cook food gently. A water bath ensures that custards are velvety and not tough, and that pâtés have a uniform texture rather than being crusty on the exterior.

## ZEST

The thin, brightly colored outer part of citrus rind. It contains volatile oils, making it ideal for use as a flavoring.

# Restaurants

Cafe Terra Cotta
4310 N Campbell Avenue
Tucson, AZ  85718-6502
520-577-8700

Tucson Country Club
2950 N Camino Principal
Tucson, AZ  85715-3199
520-298-2381

One Market/Lark Creek Inn
1 Market Street
San Francisco, CA  94105-1521
415-777-5577

Vintage Court Hotel
650 Bush Street
San Francisco, CA  94108-3509
415-392-4666

Röckenwagner
2435 Main Street
Santa Monica, CA  90405-3539
310-399-6504

i Ricchi
1220 19th Street NW
Washington, D.C.  20036-2405
202-835-0459

Le Palais du Chocolate
1200 19th Street NW
Washington, D.C.  20036-2414
202-659-4244

Le Palais du Chocolat
6925 Willow Street NW
Washington, D.C.  20012-2000
202-291-2462

Mark's Place
2286 NE 123rd Street
Miami, FL  33181-2904
305-893-6888

The Ocean Grand
Palm Beach, FL  33480
800-432-2335

1848 House
780 S Cobb Dr SE
Marietta, GA  30060-3115
770-428-1848

Elizabeth's on 37th
105 E 37th Street
Savannah, GA  31401-8611
912-236-5547

Hilton Hawaiian Village
2005 Kalia Road
Honolulu, HI  96815-1999
808-949-4321

La Mer
2199 Kalia Road
Honolulu, HI  96815-1936
808-923-2311

Grand Wailea Resort Hotel
3850 Wailea Alanui Drive
Kihea, HI  96753-8448
808-874-2355

Plantation Inn
Lahaina, HI  96761
800-433-6815

The Manele Bay Hotel
1233 Fraser Avenue
Lanai City, HI  96763
808-565-7700

Princeville Hotel
5520 Ka Haku Road
Princeville, HI  96722
808-826-9644

Four Seasons Resort Wailea
3900 Wailea Alanui Drive
Wailea, Maui, HI  96753
808-874-8000

Printer's Row Restaurant
550 S Dearborn Street
Chicago, IL  60605-1503
312-461-0780

Le Titi de Paris
1015 W Dundee Rd
Arlington Heights, IL  60004-1419
847-506-0222

Ambrosia Euro-American Patisserie
710 W Northwest Hwy
Barrington, IL  600102640
847-304-8278

Le Vichyssois
220 W IL Route 120
McHenry, IL  60050
815-385-8221

Le Francais
269 S Milwaukee Avenue
Wheeling, IL  60090-5097
847-541-7470

Lilly's
1147 Bardstown Rd
Louisville, KY  40204-1301
502-451-0447

Dakota Restaurant
629 N Highway 190
Covington, LA 70433-8961
504-892-3712

Chez Daniel
2037 Metairie Road
Metairie, LA 70005-3832
504-837-6900

Coffee Cottage
2559 Metairie Road
Metairie, LA 70001-5444
504-833-3513

Crozier's Restaurant Francais
3216 W Esplanade Ave N
Metairie, LA 70002-1667
504-833-8108

Maurice's French Pastries
3501 Hessmer Avenue
Metairie, LA 70002
504-885-1526

Bella Luna Restaurant
914 N Peters Street
New Orleans, LA 70116-3338
504-529-1583

Croissant d'Or
614 Ursulines Avenue
New Orleans, LA 70116-3204
504-524-4663

Pelican Club
312 Exchange Place
New Orleans, LA 70130-2225
504-523-1504

Palace Cafe
605 Canal Street
New Orleans, LA 70130-2307
504-523-1661

Steak Knife Restaurant
888 Harrison Avenue
New Orleans, LA 70124-3157
504-488-8981

Windsor Court Hotel
300 Gravier Street
New Orleans, LA 70130-2417
504-523-6000

The Boarding House
12 Federal Street
Nantucket, MA 02554-3568
508-228-9622

American Seasons Restaurant
80 Center Street
Nantucket, MA 02554-3604
508-228-7111

Turtle Bay Grill
118 Shawan Road
Cockeysville, MD 21030-1326
410-584-2625

Inn at Perry Cabin
308 Watkins Lane
St. Michaels, MD 21633-2114
410-745-2200

Rattlesnake Club, The
300 River Place Dr
Detroit, MI 48207-4225
313-567-4400

Franklin Street Bakery
323 Franklin Avenue
Minneapolis, MN 55404-2620
612-871-3188

Coyote Cafe
132 West Water Street
Santa Fe, NM 87501
505-983-1615

Gotham Bar and Grill
12 East 12th
New York, NY 10003
212-620-4020

JoJo's, New York, NY
160 East 64th Street
New York, NY 10021
212-223-5656

La Maison du Chocolat
25 E 73rd Street
New York, NY 10021-3521
212-744-7117

Union Square Cafe
21 E 16th St
New York, NY 10003-3104
212-243-4020

Park Avenue Cafe
100 E 63rd St
New York, NY 10021-8027
212-644-1900

French Culinary Institute
462 Broadway
New York, NY 10013-2618
212-219-8890

Le Cirque
455 Madison Avenue
New York, NY 10022-6809
212-794-9292

Fearrington House
2000 Fearrington Village Center
Pittsboro, NC 27312-8502
919-542-2121

Heathman Hotel
1001 SW Broadway
Portland, OR 97201
503-241-4100

Beaufort Inn & Restaurant
809 Port Republic Street
Beaufort, SC 29902-5550
803-521-9000

Slightly North of Broad
192 E Bay Street
Charleston, SC 29401-2171
803-723-3424

Aubergine
5007 Black Road
Memphis, TN 38117-4500
901-767-7840

Hermitage Hotel
231 6th Avenue N
Nashville. TN 37201
800-251-1908

Sunset Grill
2001 Belcourt Ave
Nashville, TN 37212-3719
615-386-3663

Cafe Annie
1728 Post Oak Blvd
Houston, TX 77056-3802
713-840-1111

Ruggles Grill
903 Westheimer Rd
Houston, TX 77006-3919
713-524-3839

Ritz-Carlton
1919 Briar Oaks Lane
Houston, TX 77027-3491
713-840-7600

Trellis Restaurant
403 Duke of Gloucester Street
Williamsburg, VA 23185
757-229-8610

L'Auberge Provencale
P.O. Box 190
White Post, VA 22663
800-638-1702

# Chefs and Cities Index

# Recipe Index